Written by

Michelle Powers, Teri Barenborg, Tari Sexton, and Lauren Monroe

Editor: Christie Weltz
Designer/Production: Kammy Peyton
Art Director: Moonhee Pak
Project Director: Stacey Faulkner

DEDICATION

This book is dedicated to all of the educators and children who have inspired us to make education a hands-on experience and, most importantly, instilled within us a lifelong love of learning.

ACKNOWLEDGMENTS

First and foremost, we would like to thank our families and friends who have supported us in so many ways—from the steadfast support of our chosen career path and passion all the way through the inspiration and creation of this series of books. Each of us has an amazing support system that has not only encouraged us but also made it possible for us to devote our time to this project. A sincere thank-you to our colleagues, both past and present, as well as all the educators who have inspired us to create a collection of lessons that encourage students to grow and take ownership of their learning. Without the continued support and encouragement of our dear friend Lynn Howard, these books would not have been possible.

Our school district, St. Lucie Public Schools, known for being the first Kids at Hope school district in the state of Florida, motivated us to build a culture of learning where students state daily that "All children are capable of success. No exceptions." This mindset, along with the work of Carol Dweck and her focus on self-efficacy through a growth mindset, has inspired us to develop lessons that encourage problem solving and perseverance, allowing students to learn from their mistakes.

We would like to thank the various teachers who have opened their doors to us and, more importantly, the students in those classrooms who have tested these exciting lessons during their development. These teachers have allowed us to model, motivate, and encourage them to transition from the "Sage on the Stage" to a "Guide on the Side," giving students the opportunity to drive their own learning.

FOREWORD

Science instruction has changed. Many of us can remember the traditional lecture and note giving model of instruction that had been used for years. I was very alone in my middle school earth science classroom and had no support, no textbook, or curriculum guide. Living day to day with content that was totally unfamiliar to me, I taught the same way to all students and didn't realize that many of them were not engaged or learning. I had to change and allow for more engagement, exploration, and experimentation. It quickly became the way I taught, and students benefited from the problem solving, collaboration, and inquiry-based activities. When I began my science teaching career years ago, I would have appreciated a resource that provided me with a set of classroom lessons that would challenge and motivate my students.

The Next Generation Science Standards are placing a great emphasis on how we "do science" in the classroom. The integration of the science, technology, engineering, arts, and math (STEAM) provides multiple opportunities to include problem solving, engineering practices, and literacy while engaging and motivating students in real-world science experiences.

I really like this book. These lessons are perfect for any teacher who may or may not feel comfortable with teaching science. I really like that the lessons are aligned with the 5E Instructional Model (engage, explore, explain, elaborate, and evaluate). Teachers who use the lessons will address the 5E model and challenge their students with the engineering process. The authors are a team of educators who understand how to teach science. Their teaching has evolved from a traditional approach to becoming facilitators of science knowledge. Teri, Lauren, Michelle, and Tari have spent time learning about the changes in science education and how to design effective science classroom environments. As a professional development associate, I spent three years with them as they explored how to create a balanced science program focused on the Next Generation Science Standards. They invested a large amount of time researching what works and implementing those best practices in their classrooms. I have had the opportunity to be in all of their classrooms and see the engagement and excitement as students collaborate on real-world engineering design problems. The teachers continually reinforce the idea that their students ARE scientists and must practice the habits of scientists. A by-product of these teachers' efforts is a book that other teachers can use today in their classrooms to make it exciting to teach and learn about science!

I am honored that Teri, Lauren, Michelle, and Tari asked me to write the foreword for their book. These teachers truly live and breathe quality science teaching and learning. Their passion, dedication, and commitment to effective science instruction make the activities and ideas in this book invaluable to anyone who wants to get excited about STEAM in their classroom.

Lynn F. Howard
Author and Professional Development Associate
Five Easy Steps to a Balanced Science Program

TABLE OF CONTENTS

INTRODUCTION

Science, technology, engineering, art, and math work together to make learning fun!

The Next Generation Science Standards place a greater emphasis on science, technology, engineering, arts, and math (STEAM) in today's classrooms. Schools are implementing and encouraging strong STEAM programs in classrooms in order to provide critical thinking lessons that meet the content standards. STEAM lessons should include problem-solving skills, enhance learning across various disciplines, promote student inquiry, and engage students with real-world situations. Students should be exposed to careers in the STEAM fields and develop skills such as communication, data analysis, following a process, designing a product, and argumentation based on evidence, all while cementing effective collaboration techniques that are necessary for a successful career in STEAM fields.

The lessons in this book are intended to support teachers in implementing the engineering design process in their classroom while integrating national standards from other disciplines. In the engineering design process, teachers become a facilitator rather than the instructional focus. Teachers encourage and guide students to work as a team to find a creative solution without providing step-by-step instructions. The engineering design process shifts away from the long-standing process of the scientific method by placing more emphasis on inquiry. Students are inspired to act as scientists and engineers through the use of sketches, diagrams, mathematical relationships, and literacy connections. By creating their very own models and products based on background information from their studies, students are immediately engaged through a meaningful, rewarding lesson.

Each lesson begins by presenting students with a design challenge scenario, or hook, in order to immediately excite students with a real-world situation that they are on a mission to solve. Students are then given a dilemma, mission, and blueprint design sheet and are asked to collaborate with team members to create several prototypes. Teams are required to choose one prototype to present to their teacher before gathering materials and constructing the chosen design. After testing out their design, teams take part in a class discussion and modify their ideas for redesign and improvement of their prototype. Finally, teams are asked to create a justification piece in order to sell their new prototype. Suggestions for justification projects are provided for each design challenge and include writing a persuasive letter, creating an advertisement or presentation, recording a video, or any other creative ideas they come up with in response to the challenge.

The engaging STEAM design challenge lessons in this book

- Promote analytical and reflective thinking
- Enhance learning across various disciplines
- Encourage students to collaborate to solve real-world design challenges
- Integrate national standards
- Are classroom tested

HOW TO USE THIS BOOK

STEAM design challenges follow the engineering practices that have become recently known in the education field. Engineering practices teach students to solve a problem by designing, creating, and justifying their design. With this model in mind, teachers shift from a "giver of information" to a "facilitator of knowledge." Instead of leading children to the right conclusion through experimental steps, the teacher allows them to work through the process themselves, often changing their plan to improve their original design.

STEAM design challenges allow art to support and enhance the learning of science and math while the engineering process is followed. Students will often use, or be encouraged to use, technology to facilitate their learning. The teacher's role as facilitator allows him or her to guide student thinking by asking questions instead of giving answers. Each lesson covers cross-curricular standards and supports teacher planning for collaboration with other teachers.

Typically, science is not taught as often in elementary school as English, reading, writing, and math, so assignments have been included within the lessons that will assist in giving students skills and practice in those other key subjects.

Lessons focus on key national science standards that are required for many standardized tests and include core English language arts and math standards. National engineering standards as well as national arts and national technology standards are also included in the lessons.

The 5E Instructional Model emphasizes building new ideas using existing knowledge. The components of this model—*Engage, Explore, Explain, Elaborate,* and *Evaluate*—are also a key design feature in the structure of each design challenge. Each design challenge requires the students to respond using mathematical, written, oral, and theatrical skills that are developmentally appropriate while working through each phase of the 5E model.

PHASES OF THE 5E MODEL

LESSON PLAN FORMAT

ENGAGE
Students make connections between past and present learning and focus their thinking on learning outcomes in the activity.

EXPLORE
Students continue to build on their knowledge of their learning through exploration and manipulation of materials.

EXPLAIN
Students support their understanding of the concepts through verbal or written communication. This is also a time when students may demonstrate new skills and when teachers can introduce new vocabulary.

ELABORATE
Students extend their understanding of concepts by obtaining more information about a topic through new experiences.

EVALUATE
Students assess their understanding of key concepts and skills.

Each lesson centers around the Design Challenge Purpose and has two distinct sections—Setting the Stage and STEAM in Action.

● Setting the Stage provides an overview of the lesson, suggested time frame, the background knowledge needed for the teacher and students as well as the standards, target vocabulary, and materials needed.

● STEAM in Action outlines the step-by-step procedure for implementing the lesson.

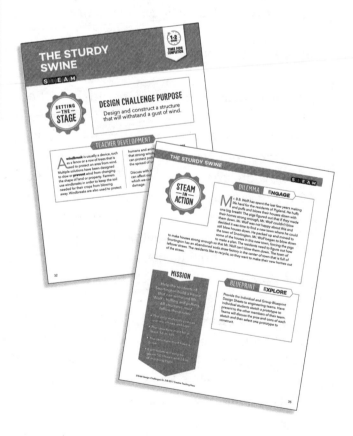

LESSON PLAN COMPONENTS

SETTING THE STAGE

Header: This section includes the title, suggested time frame for completing the lesson, and the STEAM acronym, in which the capital letters denote the main disciplines that are highlighted in each particular lesson.

Time: A suggested approximate total time for completing each lesson is provided. Because the amount of time teachers have to teach science varies within different states, districts, schools, and even grade levels, you may need to break up the lesson into smaller segments over the course of several days. Natural breaks occur between design and construction, between construction and testing, and between testing and justification.

You may choose to use the lesson ideas in the Student Development section to deepen prior knowledge or you may have your students use the literacy connections and any reputable websites you are familiar with. The lesson ideas in the Justification section are included as an optional extension of the core lesson. None of the activities before or after the core lesson are included in the time estimates. Refer to the suggested lesson timeline on page 11.

Design Challenge Purpose: This is the statement that sets the stage for the design challenge and outlines student objectives and expectations for what they should learn by completing the design challenge.

Teacher Development: This section provides background information about the science content being addressed in the lesson. Information included assists the teacher in understanding key science concepts. We understand that professional development at the elementary teacher level is often geared toward instructional delivery instead of content, especially in the content area of science. This section is provided to help support teachers who may not be as familiar with science content.

Student Development: This section contains a description of the concepts students will need to understand to complete the design challenge successfully. A link to the STEAM Dreamers website, which has active web links and additional suggested lesson ideas for deepening students' understanding of relevant science concepts, can be found on the inside front cover of this book.

Standards: This section lists specific standards for science, technology, engineering, art, math, and English language arts, along with the science and engineering practices and crosscutting concepts. These standards may apply to the activities in the challenges or in the justifications that follow. Please make sure that you review the standards for each of the lessons. The website for each set of standards is listed on page 13.

Target Vocabulary: This section lists target vocabulary to support and enhance the lesson content and to deepen students' understanding of the terms. These vocabulary terms are related to the academic content that the design challenge focuses on; can be used throughout the design challenge when in group discussion; and are an integral component of the standards covered in the challenge. Reviewing the target vocabulary prior to beginning the design challenge is recommended as students need to apply their knowledge of the science concepts and target vocabulary when solving the challenges. Ultimately, the target vocabulary should be revisited multiple times throughout the lesson.

Materials: This section lists materials and equipment that have been selected for the lessons. All materials are meant to be easy to find, inexpensive to purchase, recycled, or commonly available for free. Substitute with similar items if you have them on hand, or visit www.SteamDreamers.com for substitute suggestions.

Literacy Connections: This section lists books or articles that are meant to be used with students prior to the design challenge in order to strengthen their background knowledge and to enhance the integration of literacy in STEAM. These connections can be used during the daily classroom reading block, during small and/or whole-group instruction.

Current literacy connections for each lesson can be accessed through our website: www.SteamDreamers.com.

⚙ STEAM IN ACTION ⚙

The Dilemma: This section includes a unique real-world dilemma or scenario that hooks the students and gets them excited to solve the problem. The dilemma may include a plausible circumstance or a wild story designed to make them think. When planning the design of their prototype, student should ask themselves questions such as *Who is the client? What do we need to create? What is the purpose of the creation? What is the ultimate goal?* Students should discuss these questions with other members of their team and record their responses in their science notebooks.

Note: This is the Engage portion of the lesson, as outlined in the 5E Instructional Model.

The Mission: This section includes the defined challenge statement. This is ultimately the goal that the students are trying to reach.

Blueprint Design: This section instructs students on how to focus their thinking in order to solve the problem. Individual team members design their own plans for prototypes and list the pros and cons of their designs. Each team member reviews the Blueprint Design Sheet of every other team member and records the pros and cons he or she sees. The team then chooses which member's design it will move forward with. This is where students have the opportunity to discuss and make decisions based on their analysis on the Individual Blueprint Design Sheets. Students are allowed and encouraged to add their artistic touches to their thinking. Individual and Group Blueprint Design Sheets are found in the Appendix.

Note: This is the Explore portion of the lesson, as outlined in the 5E Instructional Model.

Engineering Design Process: In this section of the lesson, teams will take their group's selected prototype through the engineering design process to create, test, analyze, and redesign as necessary until they have successfully completed their mission.

- The first step in the process is the Engineering Task in which teams will engineer their prototype.

- Students will then test their prototype based upon the mission statement.

- The analysis of their testing will include data collection and determination of success.

- The Redesign and Retest cycle will continue until the team has successfully completed the mission.

Helpful Tips: In this section you'll find suggestions designed to address common issues that may arise during the design challenges. Some tips are geared toward the steps in the engineering design process, and some are more lesson-specific.

Reflections: This section provides suggestions for reflective questions to ask students to help guide and facilitate their thinking at various stages within the engineering design process. It is recommended that students record these questions and their reflections in a science notebook. See pages 16–19 for more information on using a science notebook.

Note: This is the Explain and Elaborate portion of the lesson, as outlined in the 5E Instructional Model.

Justification: This is the stage of the lesson where students apply what they learned in a meaningful and creative way through different mediums, such as technology and the arts. These justifications can occur in many forms: a formal letter, an advertisement, a poem, a jingle, a skit, or a technology-enhanced presentation.

Note: This is the Evaluate portion of the lesson, as outlined in the 5E Instructional Model.

SUGGESTED LESSON TIMELINE

Lesson Progression:

1. Teacher Development/Student Development/Literacy Connections

2. Dilemma/Mission/Blueprint Design

3. Engineering Task/Test Trial/Analyze/ Redesign/Reflection

4. Justification

If the lesson will be spread out over multiple days:

Day 1: Teacher Development/Student Development/Literacy Connections

Day 2: Dilemma/Mission/Blueprint Design

Day 3: Engineering Task/Test Trial

Days 4–6: Analyze/Redesign/Reflection (Can be spread over 3 days)

Days 7–8: Justification

THE APPENDIX

Lesson-Specific Activity Pages: Some lessons include specific activity pages for enhancing or completing the design challenges. They are found in the Appendix section.

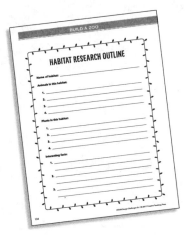

Blueprint Design Sheets: Every lesson requires students to first use the Individual Blueprint Design Sheet to create and list the pros and cons of their and their teammates' designs. Students will discuss their designs with team members and choose one design to use for building their prototype. This design, and reasons why it was chosen, are recorded on the Group Blueprint Design Sheet.

Budget Planning Chart: Any of the lessons can implement a budget for an added mathematical challenge. Prior to the start of the challenge, assign each material a cost and display for the class to reference throughout the challenge. Then decide on an overall budget for the materials. Some lessons may already provide a suggested budget. Students can use the Budget Planning Chart to itemize materials and identify the total cost of the materials needed to complete the challenge. The chart is blank to allow for more flexibility with the materials needed for specific challenges. Ensure students have a limit to what they can spend during the challenge. You can chose not to incorporate a budget if you are short on time. The time needed to assign specific material costs is not included in the overall completion time for the lessons.

Rubric: A rubric for grading the STEAM challenges is included. This rubric focuses on the engineering process. However, it does not include a means to assess the justification components.

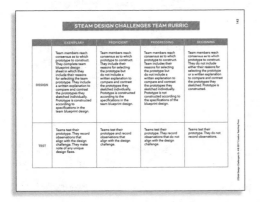

STEAM Job Cards: If your students are struggling with the collaboration process, try assigning them specific roles. Suggestions for jobs are provided on the STEAM Job Cards. Four students per team is recommended. The Accounts Manager role will only occur during the design challenges that involve a budget. In these cases, one student will have two roles, one of which is the Accounts Manager. A blank card is included to customize as necessary.

STEAM Money: The use of STEAM money is a fun way to engage students and connect the design challenges that incorporate budgets to the real world by having teams "purchase" materials. The use of STEAM money is completely optional. The following suggestions are offered should you choose to incorporate STEAM money into any of your lessons.

- Print multiple copies and laminate for durability and multiple use.

- Enlist the help of a parent volunteer to prepare the STEAM money at the beginning of the year.

- Assign material costs with the class before beginning lessons with budgets, or incorporate this into your long-range planning before school begins. This only has to be done one time. The budget is not set in stone. You may adjust the total budget amount and/or the materials cost according to students' math ability.

THE STANDARDS

SCIENCE

www.nextgenscience.org/search-standards-dci

The Next Generation Science Standards are arranged by disciplinary core ideas (DCI). When accessing these standards, search by standard and DCI. The standards are identified in the lessons by grade level and DCI. (e.g.,5-ESS3-1–Grade 5, Earth and Human Activity, Standard 1).

TECHNOLOGY

www.iste.org/standards

The International Society for Technology in Education (ISTE) publishes the national technology standards. Each of the standards is categorized into four main categories.

1. Creativity and innovation
2. Communication and collaboration
3. Research and information fluency
4. Critical thinking, problem solving, and decision making

Within each of these categories there are more specific indicators that are identified by a letter. Standards within the lessons will be indicated by the category (e.g., ISTE.1).

ENGINEERING

www.nextgenscience.org/search-standards-dci

The Next Generation Science Standards identify the engineering standards as well. They are categorized by the grade band of 3-5 (e.g., 3-5-ETS1-1).

ARTS

www.nationalartsstandards.org
www.corestandards.org/ELA-Literacy

The National Core Arts Standards are divided into four categories:

1. Creating
2. Performing/Presenting/Producing
3. Responding
4. Connecting

Each of these categories contains anchor standards. Within the lesson, the standards will be identified by the category and the anchor standard (e.g., Creating, Anchor Standard #1).

In addition to performance standards, the literacy standards are embedded throughout the lessons. Each lesson identifies specific English language arts (ELA) standards (e.g., CCSS.ELA-LITERACY.W.5.2).

MATH

www.corestandards.org/math

The Common Core Math Standards are divided into two categories:

1. Content
2. Practice

The content standards are those items such as computation and geometry. The practice standards are a framework for ensuring that students are practicing math in a meaningful and appropriate manner.

The content standards will be identified first in the Math Standards column and the Math Practice Standards will be underneath (e.g., CCSS.MATH.CONTENT.5.G.A.2–real world graphing and CCSS.MATH.PRACTICE.MP.4–model with mathematics).

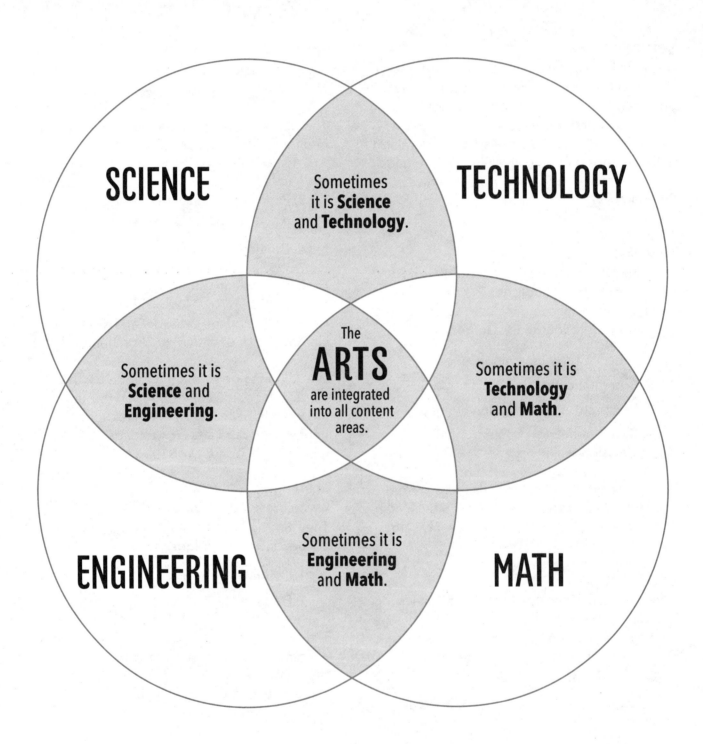

SCIENCE

TECHNOLOGY

Sometimes it is **Science** and **Technology**.

Sometimes it is **Science** and **Engineering**.

The **ARTS** are integrated into all content areas.

Sometimes it is **Technology** and **Math**.

ENGINEERING

Sometimes it is **Engineering** and **Math**.

MATH

Sometimes it is all five!

STEAM DESIGN PROCESS

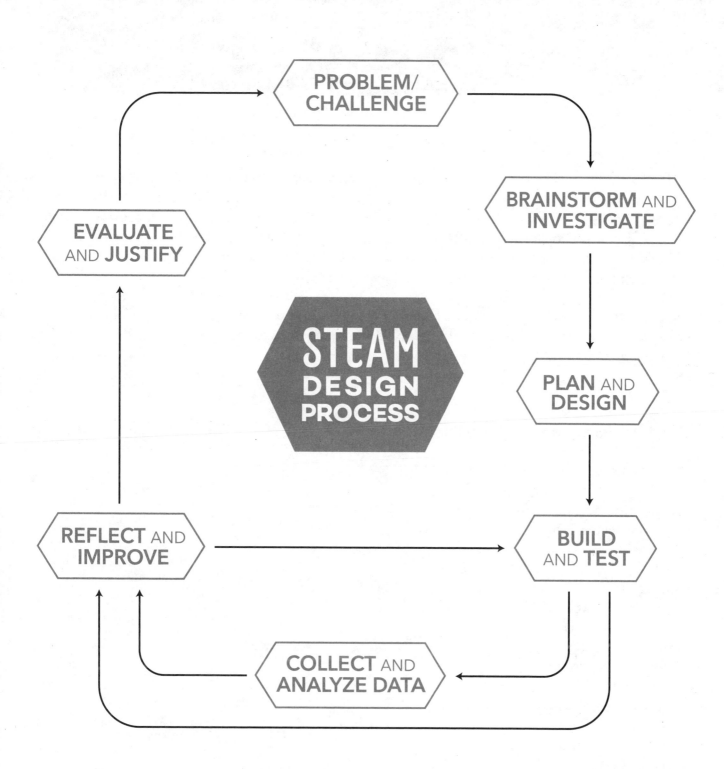

PROBLEM/
CHALLENGE

BRAINSTORM AND
INVESTIGATE

EVALUATE
AND JUSTIFY

STEAM
DESIGN
PROCESS

PLAN AND
DESIGN

REFLECT AND
IMPROVE

BUILD
AND TEST

COLLECT AND
ANALYZE DATA

RECORDING INFORMATION IN A SCIENCE NOTEBOOK

Students will record their thinking, answer questions, make observations, and sketch ideas as they work through each design challenge. It is recommended that teachers have students designate a section of their regular science notebooks to these STEAM challenges or have students create a separate STEAM science notebook using a spiral notebook, a composition book, or lined pages stapled together. A generic science notebook cover sheet has been provided in the Appendix.

Have students set up their notebooks based upon the natural breaks in the lesson. Remind students to write the name of the design challenge at the top of the page in their notebooks each time they prepare their notebooks for a new challenge.

Pages 1-3 Background Information

- Students record notes from any information provided by the teacher during whole-group instruction.

- Students record related vocabulary words and their definitions.

- Students record notes from their own independent research, including information gathered through literacy connections and existing background knowledge.

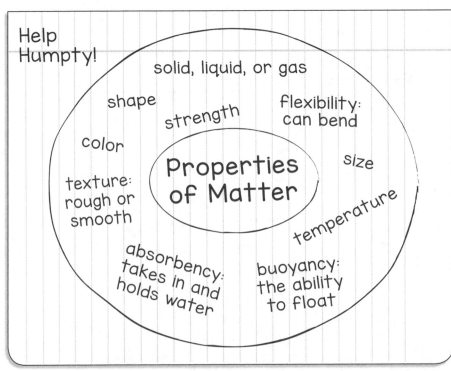

Page 1

Help Humpty!
VOCABULARY

- absorbency — the ability of an object to take in and hold water

- flexibility — an object's ability to bend without breaking

- hardness — the ability to resist changing shape

- strength — the ability to support a weight or load without breaking

- texture — describes how rough or smooth an object is

Page 2

Help Humpty!
NOTES FROM SCIENCE BOOK

p. 53 Matter
Matter is everything that you see around you. Matter is everything that has volume and takes up space.

p. 54 States of Matter
Matter is commonly found in three states. They are solid, liquid or gas. A solid object has a definite shape and a definite volume. A liquid has an indefinite shape because its shape depends on the container. But, it has a definite volume that does not change when its container changes. A gas has both an indefinite shape and an indefinite volume. It also takes the shape of its container. However, its volume will change when the container changes.

Properties of Matter
Properties of matter are the characteristics used to describe matter. They include the states of matter, color, shape, size, texture, strength, volume, weight, buoyancy, flexibility, and absorbency.

Page 3

Page 4 Dilemma and Mission

- Display the dilemma and mission for students to record.

- Or make copies of the dilemma and mission for students to glue into their notebooks to use as a reference.

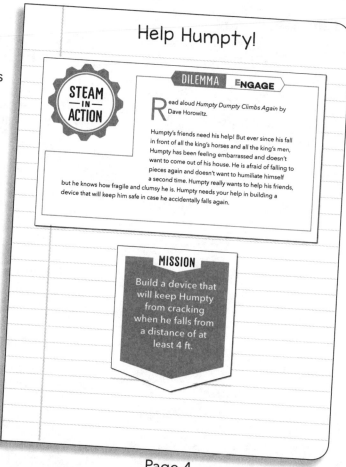

Page 4

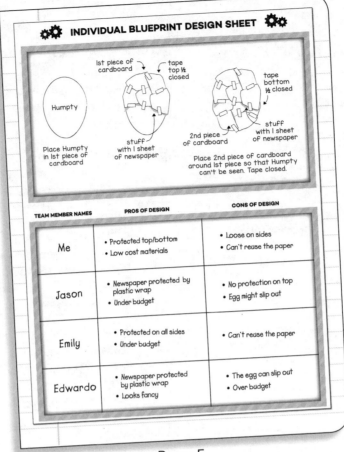

INDIVIDUAL BLUEPRINT DESIGN SHEET

TEAM MEMBER NAMES	PROS OF DESIGN	CONS OF DESIGN
Me	• Protected top/bottom • Low cost materials	• Loose on sides • Can't reuse the paper
Jason	• Newspaper protected by plastic wrap • Under budget	• No protection on top • Egg might slip out
Emily	• Protected on all sides • Under budget	• Can't reuse the paper
Edwardo	• Newspaper protected by plastic wrap • Looks fancy	• The egg can slip out • Over budget

Page 5

Page 5 Blueprint Design

● Students draw their own suggested design. Then students write the pros and cons of their and their teammates designs.

● Or make copies of the Individual Blueprint Design Sheet for students to complete and glue into their notebooks.

Help Humpty!

Help Humpty!

REFLECTIONS	EXPLAIN & ELABORATE
AFTER TEST TRIAL 1	Did your egg survive the fall without cracking? Did your prototype stay intact?
ANALYSIS	What parts of your design helped to protect the egg? What changes could you make to your prototype to make sure the egg is safe during the next fall?
AFTER TEST TRIAL 2	Did your egg and your prototype both stay intact after the fall? Did other prototypes work more effectively than yours?
ANALYSIS	What were some parts of other teams' prototypes that helped keep their eggs safe? Why did these designs work better than others?
AFTER TEST TRIAL 3	What part of your prototype could you change to keep the egg safe during a fall from a greater height? Which materials were most effective in this challenge?

Page 6

TRIAL 1

Our egg did not survive the fall even though it was protected on all sides. Our structure did well though. It did not fall apart like some of the other teams' prototypes did.
Analysis: The way our structure was made worked well. It fit together around our egg. Our newspaper is ruined and we can't use it again. We have enough money to buy two more sheets of newspaper and one sheet of plastic wrap to protect our newspaper if our egg breaks again. We won't squish our paper together. Instead of 10 cm thick, it will be 15 cm. We think this will provide more cushion.

TRIAL 2

Our egg did NOT break! Success! Two other teams were successful too. They were not more effective because we all were successful. Analysis: We all used cardboard on the outside and newspaper on the inside. The team that was not successful used plastic wrap and newspaper taped into a sort of ball, no cardboard container.

TRIAL 3

I think our container would work from a greater height. But, if I could afford more materials, I would add another layer of newspaper and another layer of cardboard.

Page 7

Pages 6-8 Engineering Task, Test Trial, Analyze, Redesign

- Students record analysis questions from the teacher and then record their answers. Or provide copies of the questions for students to glue into their notebooks.

- Record their reflections on the components of the prototypes that were successful and those that were not.

- Include additional pages as needed to allow students to record any notes, observations, and ideas as they construct and test their team prototype.

Help Humpty!

SUMMARY

Today, we learned how different properties of matter can affect objects. In this case, we were trying to protect an egg from breaking. We needed to bend the newspaper to make them the shape we needed for insulating our egg. They were flexible. We needed a strong container to protect the egg from the impact of hitting the floor. We used cardboard. Overall, our prototype was very successful because we stayed under budget and we helped keep Humpty from breaking.

Page 8

BURIED TREASURE

STEAm

SETTING —THE— STAGE

DESIGN CHALLENGE PURPOSE

Create a treasure map that includes all the parts of a map as well as different landforms.

TEACHER DEVELOPMENT

This challenge asks students to create a model that includes landforms. **Models** are used when something is too large or too expensive for scientists to study. A **map** is a model that represents a real place.

A **physical map** includes features such as lakes, mountains, rivers, and forests. In order to meet the standards, teams will need to be specific and detailed when they create their treasure maps.

BURIED TREASURE

STUDENT DEVELOPMENT

Review the concepts of models, landforms, and the parts of a map (e.g., title, scale, compass rose, and key) to prepare for this challenge.

Lesson Idea: Play pictionary! In advance, prepare a set of cards for each group by writing the name of a different landform (e.g., *lake*, *river*, *forest*, or *mountain*) on

each card. Place students into groups of four. Place the stack of cards facedown. Students will take turns choosing a card, not showing it to anyone, and drawing a picture of the landform to get his or her team members to correctly identify it. As an added challenge, set a timer and have teams try to correctly identify all the cards in the pile before time runs out.

STANDARDS

SCIENCE	TECHNOLOGY	ENGINEERING	ARTS	MATH	ELA
2-ESS2-2		K-2-ETS1-1	Creating #1		CCSS.ELA-LITERACY.W.2.3
		K-2-ETS1-2	Creating #2		
		K-2-ETS1-3	Creating #3		

SCIENCE & ENGINEERING PRACTICES

Developing and Using Models: Develop a model to represent patterns in the natural world.

CROSSCUTTING CONCEPTS

Patterns: Patterns in the natural world can be observed.

Stability and Change: Things may change slowly or rapidly.

TARGET VOCABULARY

compass rose

key (on map)

landform

map

model

physical map

scale (on map)

title (on map)

MATERIALS

- white paper
- sticky notes
- colored pencils
- rulers
- markers
- gold coins
- brown paper bag cut apart or brown craft paper
- various maps for reference

Note: Make this mission more challenging by providing several reference maps of different areas. Make it less challenging by giving the same reference map to each team.

LITERACY CONNECTIONS

How I Became a Pirate by Melinda Long

NOTES

DILEMMA — ENGAGE

The great pirate Captain Plunderloot and his crew have entrusted you with their treasure chest. They've even made you an honorary pirate! But they need your help in return. They want you to find the perfect spot to bury their treasure. They've given you several maps to use as a reference to get ideas about the things you can include on your map. However, Captain Plunderloot insists that there be no names or labels on the map. Instead, he wants you to write descriptions of the landforms and features on your map. Can you use the reference map from the captain to create your own map to the buried treasure?

MISSION

Use the reference map provided by Captain Plunderloot to help you create a treasure map. Include the parts of a map and descriptions of the landforms and features on your map as clues to the location of the treasure. Do not include the name of the landforms or features. Mark your treasure map with an X to show where the treasure is buried.

BLUEPRINT — EXPLORE

Provide the Individual and Group Blueprint Design Sheets to engineering teams. Have individual students sketch a prototype to present to the other members of their team. Teams will discuss the pros and cons of each sketch and then select one prototype to construct.

ENGINEERING TASK

Using a map as a reference, each team will create its own treasure map that includes the parts of a map and different landforms. Teams should not label the landforms or features on their maps. Instead, they should write descriptions of the landforms as clues for the location of the treasure. Teams will mark the location of the treasure on the reference map with a sticky note.

TEST TRIAL

Each team will try to find another team's buried treasure by using that team's treasure map. Once the team believes it knows where the treasure is located, the team will mark the location with a sticky note and take it to the teacher to check for accuracy. If the team is correct, it receives a gold coin.

Teams will each leave one positive comment and one suggestion about the other team's map on a sticky note.

ANALYZE

Teams will discuss the comments left on the sticky notes attached to their maps. They will reflect on what changes they should make.

REDESIGN

Teams will use colored pencils to make changes to their treasure maps to improve the clues or appearance of the landforms on their maps.

Note: Have teams transfer their final map onto brown paper after test trial 2 for an authentic treasure map feel.

HELPFUL TIPS

- After the Test Trial, have teams take a gallery walk to view other teams' designs for possible ideas to assist them in the Analyze and Redesign portions of the engineering design process.

- If teams are successful on the first try, encourage them to make their prototypes even more efficient. If it is a scenario in which this is not feasible, distribute team members to other teams to be a support for them in making their prototypes more efficient. Alternatively, at teacher discretion, move students on to the Justification portion of the lesson.

- If after the third test the final prototype is still unsuccessful, have students write how they would start over. These challenges are meant to have students build on what they originally designed. If the design proved to be unsuccessful, encourage a reflection or justification on what they would do if they were allowed to start again from scratch.

REFLECTIONS EXPLAIN & ELABORATE

AFTER TEST TRIAL 1	Were you able to find any of the other teams´ buried treasure? What features on the map helped you find the treasure chest? Did any of the other teams find your treasure?
ANALYSIS	What changes will you make to your map? What landforms will you add?
AFTER TEST TRIAL 2	Were you able to find any of the other teams´ buried treasure? What features on the map helped you find the treasure chest? Did any of the other teams find your treasure?
ANALYSIS	What changes will you make to your map? What landforms will you add?
AFTER TEST TRIAL 3	Did you recreate your map on brown paper? Does it look more like a real treasure map? What landforms were the easiest to model on your treasure map? What landforms were the easiest to read on your treasure map?

JUSTIFICATION EVALUATE

ELA	Write a narrative story about your experience as an honorary pirate.
ARTS	Design and create your own treasure chest using a shoebox and art materials.

PROTECT THE MARINA

SETTING —THE— STAGE

DESIGN CHALLENGE PURPOSE

Design and build a barrier that will protect a boat marina.

TEACHER DEVELOPMENT

This lesson is designed to help students understand that wind and water can shape the land. **Weathering** breaks down rock into sediment, while **erosion** is the process of the sediment being carried away. In the dilemma for this challenge, the beach is weathered by the waves caused by the force of wind. Erosion takes place as the sand is moved to a different location.

In this challenge, students will build a **windbreak** (trees, shrubs, or screen that provide shelter from the wind) to help prevent the capsizing of the boats. In the reflection questions, they will be asked to note their observations regarding any difference in the shape of the beach in the protected and unprotected areas following the testing.

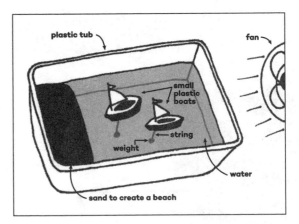

plastic tub

fan

small plastic boats

string

weight

water

sand to create a beach

STEAM

STUDENT DEVELOPMENT

In order for students to be successful in this challenge, they will need to have a basic understanding of how water can shape and form land. Its force is powerful. When wind is added to the situation, the force is that much more powerful. A hurricane is a type of weather that has strong winds and rain. If students aren't familiar with hurricanes, describing nor'easters, snowstorms, and bad thunderstorms over water can help students with the background knowledge that they need to understand why a marina needs protection from the wind.

Lesson Idea: Find a student with longer hair to be your helper. Ask students to describe what they notice about the helper's hair when there is no wind. Put a fan/blow dryer in a position that would move the hair, and change the speeds to allow students to see the various forces of the wind. Ask students to describe the difference.

Note: Visit the website listed on the inside front cover for more information about weather in your region.

STANDARDS

SCIENCE	TECHNOLOGY	ENGINEERING	ARTS	MATH	ELA
2-ESS2-1		K-2-ETS1-1	Creating #1	CCSS.MATH. CONTENT.2.MD.A.1	CCSS.ELA-LITERACY.W.2.2
		K-2-ETS1-2		CCSS.MATH. CONTENT.2.MD.A.4	
		K-2-ETS1-3			

SCIENCE & ENGINEERING PRACTICES

Asking questions and defining problems: Define a simple problem that can be solved through the development of a new or improved object or tool.

Developing and using models: Develop and/or use models to describe and/or predict phenomena.

CROSSCUTTING CONCEPTS

Cause and Effect: Events have causes that generate observable patterns.

Structure and Function: The shape and stability of structures of natural and designed objects are related to their function(s).

TARGET VOCABULARY

barrier

gust

marina

wave

windbreak

MATERIALS

- disposable aluminum roasting pan filled with water (just enough for the boats to float)
- sand (represents the beach)
- small toy boats with "anchors" (string with metal washers attached)
- fan or blow dryer (represents hurricane wind)
- wax paper
- clay
- pebbles
- craft sticks
- ruler

Note: Have students first build their barriers on wax paper and then move the barrier to the tub for testing.

LITERACY CONNECTIONS

The Magic School Bus Inside a Hurricane by Joanna Cole

Hurricanes! by Gail Gibbons

NOTES

STEAM —IN— ACTION

DILEMMA — ENGAGE

Captain Barge is a local fisherman who lives in the coastal town of Bluewater. The town is surrounded by a forest. Bluewater has many beautiful boat marinas where the fishermen keep their boats. Last night, Captain Barge was listening to the weather forecast, and it said that Bluewater will be hit with five hurricanes this year! The marinas of Bluewater do not have any protection from winds created by a hurricane. Captain Barge needs you to design a windbreak to help protect the boats in the marina. Can you help him?

MISSION

Create a barrier prototype that will protect the boat marina. The barrier must be at least 10 cm shorter than the marina (testing tub) in order for boats to have a passageway to open waters.

BLUEPRINT — EXPLORE

Provide the Individual and Group Blueprint Design Sheets to engineering teams. Have individual students sketch a prototype to present to the other members of their team. Teams will discuss the pros and cons of each sketch and then select one prototype to construct.

Note: Students will need to make note of the length of their prototype compared to the length of the marina.

ENGINEERING TASK

Each team will design and build a barrier to protect boats in the marina against the hurricane winds for one minute.

TEST TRIAL

After a team places its barrier in front of the marina, wind from the fan will push the water against the barrier for one minute to test the barrier's effectiveness.

Before the test, teams will need to confirm that their barriers are at least 10 cm shorter than the marina.

ANALYZE

Teams will observe how much water went over the barrier and record notes about how many boats were affected by the wind.

Teams should be allowed to observe the other designs to gather ideas, reflect, and make changes to improve their prototypes.

REDESIGN

Teams can use a colored pencil to make adjustments to their original design sketches. Then they can get new supplies if needed to rebuild and retest their prototypes.

HELPFUL TIPS

- After the Test Trial, have teams take a gallery walk to view other teams' designs for possible ideas to assist them in the Analyze and Redesign portions of the engineering design process.

- If teams are successful on the first try, encourage them to make their prototypes even more efficient. If it is a scenario in which this is not feasible, distribute team members to other teams to be a support for them in making their prototypes more efficient. Alternatively, at teacher discretion, move students on to the Justification portion of the lesson.

- If after the third test the final prototype is still unsuccessful, have students write how they would start over. These challenges are meant to have students build on what they originally designed. If the design proved to be unsuccessful, encourage a reflection or justification on what they would do if they were allowed to start again from scratch.

STEAM Design Challenges Gr. 2 © 2017 Creative Teaching Press

STEAM

REFLECTIONS — EXPLAIN & ELABORATE

AFTER TEST TRIAL 1	Did water get past your barrier? Why do you think that happened? Are there any differences between the protected and unprotected areas of the beach?
ANALYSIS	What changes can you make to be sure your barrier protects the boats in the marina?
AFTER TEST TRIAL 2	After making the changes, did your barrier protect the marina? What differences do you observe between the area of the beach protected by the barrier and the area that is not?
ANALYSIS	If you could change the materials you used to create your barrier, would you? What materials would you use instead? Why?
AFTER TEST TRIAL 3	Did your barrier keep the boats in the marina safe?
ANALYSIS	How did your barrier compare with the other teams' barriers? Did your barrier keep the boats safe in the marina? Describe the changes you observed in the shape of the beach.

JUSTIFICATION — EVALUATE

ELA — Write an explanatory text describing how your team chose to build your barrier for Captain Barge and the town of Bluewater.

ARTS — Design a sign advertising the safety precautions that the marina took to keep the boats safe.

THE STURDY SWINE

SETTING —THE— STAGE

DESIGN CHALLENGE PURPOSE

Design and construct a structure that will withstand a gust of wind.

TEACHER DEVELOPMENT

A windbreak is a natural or man-made object, such as a fence or a row of trees, that protects an area from wind. Multiple solutions have been designed to slow or prevent wind from changing the shape of land or property. Farmers use windbreaks in order to keep the soil needed for their crops from blowing away. Windbreaks are also used to protect humans and animals from the damage that strong winds can cause. Windbreaks can protect pollination as well as prevent the spread of unwanted pesticides.

Discuss with students the many ways wind can affect our environment and ways in which we can help protect against future damage.

STUDENT DEVELOPMENT

Discuss vocabulary terms and review with students how to use a ruler to **measure** the **length** of an object using appropriate tools, such as rulers, yardsticks, metersticks, and measuring tapes. Allow students to practice measuring and recording the length of classroom objects before starting this lesson.

Discuss the remaining target vocabulary terms and their meanings. **Outskirts** are the borders surrounding an area. The term **prevent** means to stop something from happening. A **windbreak** is a shelter used to protect an area from damaging winds.

Have students recount the story of "The Three Little Pigs," discussing the details of how the houses were destroyed.

STANDARDS

SCIENCE	TECHNOLOGY	ENGINEERING	ARTS	MATH	ELA
2-ESS2-1		K-2-ETS1-1	Creating #1	CCSS.MATH. CONTENT 2.MD.A.1	CCSS.ELA-LITERACY.W.2.3
		K-2-ETS1-2	Creating #2	CCSS.MATH. CONTENT 2.MD.B.6	CCSS.ELA-LITERACY.SL.2.4
		K-2-ETS1-3	Creating #3		

SCIENCE & ENGINEERING PRACTICES

Constructing Explanations and Designing Solutions: Compare multiple solutions to a problem.

CROSSCUTTING CONCEPTS

Stability and Change: Things may change slowly or rapidly.

TARGET VOCABULARY

length

measure

outskirts

prevent

windbreak

MATERIALS

- fan (to simulate wind from Mr. Wolf)

- 24 in. of masking tape

- 50 straws

- ruler

LITERACY CONNECTIONS

The Three Little Pigs by Parragon Books

The Three Little Javelinas by Susan Lowell

No Lie, Pigs (and Their Houses) Can Fly!: The Story of the Three Little Pigs as Told by the Wolf by Jessica Gunderson

NOTES

STEAM —IN— ACTION

DILEMMA   ENGAGE

Mr. B.B. Wolf has spent the last few years making life hard for the residents of Pigland. He huffs and puffs and blows their houses down with one big breath! The pigs figured out that if they made their homes strong enough, Mr. Wolf couldn't blow them down. Mr. Wolf was not happy about this and decided it was time to find a new town where he could still blow houses down. He packed up and moved to the town of Snortington. Mr. Wolf began to blow down some of the houses in this new town, forcing the pigs to make a plan. The residents need to figure out how to make houses strong enough so that Mr. Wolf can't blow them down. The town of Snortington has an abandoned soda straw factory in the center of town that is full of leftover straws. The residents like to recycle, so they want to make their new homes out of the straws.

MISSION

Help the residents of Snortington build a house that can withstand Mr. Wolf's huffing and puffing. All structures must follow these rules:

- The only materials you can use are straws and tape.

- The structure must be at least 16 in. tall.

- The structure must have a base.

- Each team will only be given 50 straws and 24 in. of masking tape.

BLUEPRINT   EXPLORE

Provide the Individual and Group Blueprint Design Sheets to engineering teams. Have individual students sketch a prototype to present to the other members of their team. Teams will discuss the pros and cons of each sketch and then select one prototype to construct.

ENGINEERING TASK

Each team will design and construct a new house prototype for the residents of Snortington.

TEST TRIAL

Each engineering team will test its structure by placing it in front of the fan for 20 seconds to determine if it will withstand Mr. Wolf's huffing and puffing.

ANALYZE

Facilitate analytical discussions comparing the structures and designs of the different prototypes.

Teams should be allowed to observe the other designs to gather ideas, reflect, and make changes in order to improve their prototypes.

REDESIGN

Teams can use a colored pencil to make adjustments to their original design sketches. Then they can get new supplies if needed to rebuild and retest their prototypes.

 # HELPFUL TIPS

- After the Test Trial, have teams take a gallery walk to view other teams' designs for possible ideas to assist them in the Analyze and Redesign portions of the engineering design process.

- If teams are successful on the first try, encourage them to make their prototypes even more efficient. If it is a scenario in which this is not feasible, distribute team members to other teams to be a support for them in making their prototypes more efficient. Alternatively, at teacher discretion, move students on to the Justification portion of the lesson.

- If after the third test the final prototype is still unsuccessful, have students write how they would start over. These challenges are meant to have students build on what they originally designed. If the design proved to be unsuccessful, encourage a reflection or justification on what they would do if they were allowed to start again from scratch.

REFLECTIONS **E**XPLAIN & **E**LABORATE

AFTER TEST TRIAL 1	When Mr. Wolf huffed and puffed, did your structure stay standing? Did other teams design structures that stayed standing?
ANALYSIS	What were some of the similarities and differences between the structures? What changes will you make to your prototype to make it more sturdy?
AFTER TEST TRIAL 2	Did your structure remain standing after Mr. Wolf huffed and puffed?
ANALYSIS	Why do you think some structures were more sturdy than others? What do you need to adjust on your structure to make it more sturdy?
AFTER TEST TRIAL 3	How many structures were sturdy enough to stay standing when Mr. Wolf huffed and puffed? If you could start over, what would your team do differently to make your structure stronger?

JUSTIFICATION **E**VALUATE

ELA	Write a friendly letter to the pigs of Snortington from the point of view of Mr. Wolf. Explain why you should be allowed to stay in town. Include details to describe actions, thoughts, and feelings. Use temporal words and phrases, such as *first*, *next*, and *finally*, to signal event order and provide a sense of closure.
ARTS	*Note*: Students will need a copy of the wanted poster outline on page 129. Use the wanted poster to help catch Mr. Wolf.

THIS MODEL FLOWS!

STEAm

2 HOURS

TIME FOR COMPLETION

SETTING —THE— STAGE

DESIGN CHALLENGE PURPOSE

Build a model of a log chute ride for the Natural Fun Water Park Company.

TEACHER DEVELOPMENT

If students have never made a model before, you will need to either show a video or give an example of how to make a model of a real environment.

Models are used in a science classroom to allow students to conceptualize something that they can't physically measure because of its size. For example, second graders probably can't measure the dimensions of a lake. However, they can measure a model of a lake in order to better understand its features.

Students may need support in understanding how to create a realistic model using clay. Demonstrate for students how to create the defining features of different landforms. This could include the use of thumbs to make depressions in the banks of a model lake or pinching the clay to show the rocks found in a model stream.

Note: Visit the website listed on the inside front cover for more information about using models to deepen understanding of concepts.

THIS MODEL FLOWS!

STEAM

STUDENT DEVELOPMENT

Students will need background information on the different bodies of water and related landforms, such as lakes, rivers, and waterfalls. Students will also need to know what log chute rides look like and how the logs travel along the routes. Students should also have experience observing objects floating and moving in water. Previous experience using modeling clay will also help students as they design and build their water park rides for this challenge.

Note: Visit the website listed on the inside front cover for more information about bodies of water and related landforms. The site also includes videos and images of log chute rides.

STANDARDS

SCIENCE	TECHNOLOGY	ENGINEERING	ARTS	MATH	ELA
2-ESS2-2		K-2-ETS1-1	Creating #1		CCSS.ELA-LITERACY.SL.2.4
		K-2-ETS1-2	Creating #2		CCSS.ELA-LITERACY.W.2.3
		K-2-ETS1-3	Creating #3		

SCIENCE & ENGINEERING PRACTICES

Developing and Using Models: Develop a model to represent patterns in the natural world.

CROSSCUTTING CONCEPTS

Patterns: Patterns in the natural world can be observed.

TARGET VOCABULARY

canyon

lake

model

river

waterfall

MATERIALS

- disposable aluminum roasting pan (or other similar size container)
- clay
- toothpicks
- water source
- This Model Flows Rubric (page 130)
- map (page 131)

LITERACY CONNECTIONS

Grand Canyon Vacation Trip: What to See by Steven Wilson

Waterfalls by Mari Schuh and Gail Saunders-Smith

Rivers by Alyse Sweeney

Follow the Water from Brook to Ocean by Arthur Dorros

NOTES

STEAM —IN— ACTION

DILEMMA | ENGAGE

Mr. Agua, the president of the Natural Fun Water Park Company, wants to build a new water park. The park rides need to look like they are in a real environment and must include different examples of bodies of water and related landforms. The park needs a log chute ride that allows guests to travel in a log across a lake, onto a river, through a canyon, and over a waterfall. The ride must look like it belongs in the real world and must include a labeled map guests can look at during the ride that informs them about the different bodies of water and landforms they encounter throughout the ride. Mr. Agua needs teams of engineers to build models of the ride. The model ride that meets all of the requirements, including a map that identifies the bodies of water and landforms that the ride travels through, will be made into a ride at Mr. Agua's new water park.

MISSION

Create a model of a log chute ride that meets the following requirements:

- The log must travel through a canyon, lake, river, and over a waterfall.

- Include a labeled map that identifies each body of water and landform.

BLUEPRINT | EXPLORE

Provide the Individual and Group Blueprint Design Sheets to engineering teams. Have individual students sketch a prototype to present to the other members of their team. Teams will discuss the pros and cons of each sketch and then select one prototype to construct.

ENGINEERING TASK	TEST TRIAL	ANALYZE	REDESIGN
Each team will build a model of a log chute ride with bodies of water and landforms represented. Include a map labeling the bodies of water and landforms. *Note:* Maps should show where the ride starts and stops and include labels for all landforms and bodies of water.	Teams will test their model log chute rides by adding water and floating toothpick logs down the model. The teacher will use the rubric to ensure teams meet all of the challenge requirements. *Note:* To ensure that the toothpick doesn't stick to the walls of the model, have the students put a small ball of clay on each end to act as bumpers.	Teams will review their rubric results to see if they fulfilled all of the requirements. Teams should be allowed to observe the other designs to gather ideas, reflect, and make changes in order to improve their models.	Teams can use a colored pencil to make adjustments to their original design sketches. Then they can get new supplies if needed to rebuild and retest their prototypes.

HELPFUL TIPS

- After the Test Trial, have teams take a gallery walk to view other teams' designs for possible ideas to assist them in the Analyze and Redesign portions of the engineering design process.

- If teams are successful on the first try, encourage them to make their prototypes even more efficient. If it is a scenario in which this is not feasible, distribute team members to other teams to be a support for them in making their prototypes more efficient. Alternatively, at teacher discretion, move students on to the Justification portion of the lesson.

- If after the third test the final prototype is still unsuccessful, have students write how they would start over. These challenges are meant to have students build on what they originally designed. If the design proved to be unsuccessful, encourage a reflection or justification on what they would do if they were allowed to start again from scratch.

THIS MODEL FLOWS!

REFLECTIONS — EXPLAIN & ELABORATE

AFTER TEST TRIAL 1	Did your log (toothpick) travel down the entire length of your model? Were all of the required bodies of water and landforms represented?
ANALYSIS	Did your log (toothpick) travel across a lake and river and down waterfall? Did it travel through a canyon? What can you do to your model to improve it so that your log travels through all of the bodies of water and landforms?
AFTER TEST TRIAL 2	Did your map look like your model? Did your log travel through all of the required bodies of water and landforms?
ANALYSIS	Do you need to improve your map so that it looks like your model?
AFTER TEST TRIAL 3	Did your model work? Does your map correctly represent your model?

JUSTIFICATION — EVALUATE

ELA
Imagine your model is a real environment. Write a story about the log as it travels through the bodies of water and landforms of your model. Include details about the river, lake, canyon, and waterfall.

ARTS
Give your ride a name, and create a poster to advertise it.

BLAZING BOOKS

sTEAM

SETTING
—THE—
STAGE

DESIGN CHALLENGE PURPOSE

Build a zip line that carries an object across a space of at least 10 ft. and drops the object onto a target before reaching the opposite end of the zip line.

TEACHER DEVELOPMENT

The lesson requires students to apply the steps of the engineering design process to complete the challenge.

Refer to the diagram of the STEAM design process (page 15) for a description of each step.

STUDENT DEVELOPMENT

This is a great lesson for teaching the engineering process to students. Introduce the words **blueprint**, **design**, **engineer**, and **prototype** to your students. Teach them how to collaborate and work as a team. Use the STEAM job cards (page 145) to assign jobs to students to demonstrate the importance of working together

STANDARDS

SCIENCE	TECHNOLOGY	ENGINEERING	ARTS	MATH	ELA
	ISTE.2	K-2-ETS1-1	Creating #1	CCSS.MATH. CONTENT.2.MD.A.1	CCSS.ELA-LITERACY.W.2.2
		K-2-ETS1-2	Creating #2		
		K-2-ETS1-3	Creating #3		

SCIENCE & ENGINEERING PRACTICES

Asking Questions and Defining Problems: Ask questions based on observations to find more information about the natural and/or designed world.

Define a simple problem that can be solved through the development of a new or improved object or tool.

Developing and Using Models: Develop a simple model based on evidence to represent a proposed object or tool.

Analyzing and Interpreting Data: Analyze data from tests of an object or tool to determine if it works as intended.

CROSSCUTTING CONCEPTS

Structure and Function: The shape and stability of structures of natural and designed objects are related to their function(s).

TARGET VOCABULARY

blueprint

design

prototype

ravine

zip line

MATERIALS

- 9 ft. of fishing line
- 1 index card
- 1 small paper cup
- 1 marble
- masking tape
- paper clips
- scissors
- colored pencil
- 1 sheet of construction paper (the target)

LITERACY CONNECTIONS

Clara and the Book Wagon
by Nancy Smiler Levinson

NOTES

STEAM
—IN—
ACTION

DILEMMA | ENGAGE

Your best friend, Ree Mote, and her family just moved to an area across the ravine from where you live. Her parents are researching animals native to that area and have taken her along. She's desperate for something to do. She has no Internet connection, and there is no TV or cell phone signal. It takes over two hours to get back to town from her current location, and she doesn't want to interrupt her parents' important work. Ree needs you to send her some books to read. Build a zip line that will carry the books across the ravine and drop them in Ree's front yard.

MISSION

Create a zip line that will carry a marble from your location and drop it onto a target.

BLUEPRINT | EXPLORE

Provide the Individual and Group Blueprint Design Sheets to engineering teams. Have individual students sketch a prototype to present to the other members of their team. Teams will discuss the pros and cons of each sketch and then select one prototype to construct.

ENGINEERING TASK → **TEST TRIAL** → **ANALYZE** → **REDESIGN**

ENGINEERING TASK	TEST TRIAL	ANALYZE	REDESIGN
Each team will build a zip line that carries a marble across an open space of at least 10 ft. and then drops the marble onto a target before reaching the end of the line.	Teams will test their prototypes and record their observations. Teams should measure and record the distance from their target to the location where the marble landed.	Teams will analyze the results of the test and determine what changes to make to their prototypes. Teams should be allowed to observe the other designs to gather ideas, reflect, and make changes in order to improve their prototypes.	Teams can use a colored pencil to make adjustments to their original design sketches. Then they can get new supplies if needed to rebuild and retest their prototypes.

 HELPFUL TIPS

- After the Test Trial, have teams take a gallery walk to view other teams' designs for possible ideas to assist them in the Analyze and Redesign portions of the engineering design process.

- If teams are successful on the first try, encourage them to make their prototypes even more efficient. If it is a scenario in which this is not feasible, distribute team members to other teams to be a support for them in making their prototypes more efficient. Alternatively, at teacher discretion, move students on to the Justification portion of the lesson.

- If after the third test the final prototype is still unsuccessful, have students write how they would start over. These challenges are meant to have students build on what they originally designed. If the design proved to be unsuccessful, encourage a reflection or justification on what they would do if they were allowed to start again from scratch.

(S)TEAM

REFLECTIONS EXPLAIN & ELABORATE

AFTER TEST TRIAL 1	Which team's prototype was closest to hitting the target? Did your team's prototype hit the target? How far from the target did your marble land?
ANALYSIS	What changes will you make to your prototype? Explain.
AFTER TEST TRIAL 2	What were some of the similarities and differences between the prototypes? Which team was closest to hitting its target? How far from the target did your marble land? How much closer was your prototype to hitting the target after you made changes to your design?
ANALYSIS	What changes will you make to your zip line? Explain.
AFTER TEST TRIAL 3	Which team's prototype was most effective at hitting the target? Was your team's prototype successful at hitting the target?

JUSTIFICATION EVALUATE

TECHNOLOGY	Use the Internet to research zip lines. Create a slideshow about zip lines, and include information about their origin and their use today.
ELA	Write an informational paragraph about zip lines.
ARTS	Create a detailed diagram of a zip line. Label its parts.

CANDY CORN CATAPULT

STEAM

SETTING —THE— STAGE

DESIGN CHALLENGE PURPOSE

Design a catapult that launches an object at a target 10 ft. away.

TEACHER DEVELOPMENT

In this activity, students will be using unbalanced forces to move an object across a distance of 10 ft. **Movement** is when an object has a change of position. It is also a result of **unbalanced forces**. A **force** is a push or a pull. When we use force to move an object, we are applying more force than whatever forces are holding it in place. Think of a tug-of-war contest. When both sides are applying the same amount of force, the rope doesn't move.

However, when one side pulls with more force than the other, the rope moves toward the side applying more force.

A **catapult** was an ancient weapon used for throwing large rocks. Catapults are used today for different things, including as a device for **launching** a jet from the deck of an aircraft carrier. In this challenge, students will create a device that launches a piece of candy corn across a distance of 10 ft.

STUDENT DEVELOPMENT

You may want to review the term **launch** with your students. Discuss what tools people use to launch objects across distances. Talk about catapults and compare them to slingshots.

Lesson Idea: Hold a tug-of-war contest. Try to balance the sides so that there is very little rope movement. Have some adult volunteers join one of the sides. Discuss the results with students.

STANDARDS

SCIENCE	TECHNOLOGY	ENGINEERING	ARTS	MATH	ELA
		K-2-ETS1-1	Creating #1	CCSS.MATH. CONTENT.2.OA.A.1	CCSS.ELA-LITERACY.SL.2.1
		K-2-ETS1-2	Creating #2		CCSS.ELA-LITERACY.W.2.1
		K-2-ETS1-3	Creating #3		

SCIENCE & ENGINEERING PRACTICES

Asking Questions and Defining Problems: Define a simple problem that can be solved through the development of a new or improved object or tool.

Analyzing and Interpreting Data: Analyze data from tests of an object or tool to determine if it works as intended.

CROSSCUTTING CONCEPTS

Structure and Function: The shape and stability of structures of natural and designed objects are related to their function(s).

TARGET VOCABULARY

catapult

force

launch

motion

MATERIALS

- plastic spoons
- craft sticks
- rubber bands
- pencils
- empty tissue box
- tape
- small paper cups
- empty cereal box
- string
- candy corn
- paper plate
- markers
- meterstick

LITERACY CONNECTIONS

The Adventures of The Ketchup Kids by Andrew Burton

NOTES

STEAM
—IN—
ACTION

DILEMMA   ENGAGE

Harvestville's annual fall festival is coming up in two weeks. Members of the town have been working diligently to set up all of the food and carnival stands so that families can enjoy this special weekend of fun. Your elementary school has been given the task of creating a pumpkin-launching catapult as one of the new main attractions. The most effective pumpkin-launching prototype will be used as a model for building the real catapult used in the festival. The team with the most effective pumpkin catapult will gain free entry to the festival for all team members.

MISSION

Design and construct a catapult to launch a piece of candy corn 10 ft. to hit a target.

BLUEPRINT   EXPLORE

Provide the Individual and Group Blueprint Design Sheets to engineering teams. Have individual students sketch a prototype to present to the other members of their team. Teams will discuss the pros and cons of each sketch and then select one prototype to construct.

ENGINEERING TASK	TEST TRIAL	ANALYZE	REDESIGN
Each team will construct a catapult that can launch a piece of candy corn and hit a target 10 ft. away.	Teams will test their catapults by launching candy corn at a paper plate target located 10 ft. from the launching point. Each team will be allowed three trials. *Note:* For an added challenge, use a marker to divide the paper plate into sections with each section representing a different point value. Allow teams to keep track of their point total during each test trial.	Teams will measure and record the distance the candy corn traveled and make observations about each team's trials. Teams should be allowed to observe the other designs to gather ideas, reflect, and make changes in order to improve their prototypes.	Teams can use a colored pencil to make adjustments to their original design sketches. Then they can get new supplies if needed to rebuild and retest their prototypes.

HELPFUL TIPS

- After the Test Trial, have teams take a gallery walk to view other teams' designs for possible ideas to assist them in the Analyze and Redesign portions of the engineering design process.

- If teams are successful on the first try, encourage them to make their prototypes even more efficient. If it is a scenario in which this is not feasible, distribute team members to other teams to be a support for them in making their prototypes more efficient. Alternatively, at teacher discretion, move students on to the Justification portion of the lesson.

- If after the third test the final prototype is still unsuccessful, have students write how they would start over. These challenges are meant to have students build on what they originally designed. If the design proved to be unsuccessful, encourage a reflection or justification on what they would do if they were allowed to start again from scratch.

REFLECTIONS — EXPLAIN & ELABORATE

AFTER TEST TRIAL 1	Did your catapult launch the candy corn 10 ft.? Did the candy corn hit the target?
ANALYSIS	What design changes made it possible for your catapult to launch the candy corn the distance it traveled? What did you notice about the differences in other designs?
AFTER TEST TRIAL 2	Was your catapult more accurate this time around? Did the candy corn travel a greater distance?
ANALYSIS	Did the changes you made to your design help the candy corn hit the target? What else can you change to increase the accuracy of your catapult?
AFTER TEST TRIAL 3	Which parts of your design were most effective? Would you change any other part of your design in the future?

JUSTIFICATION — EVALUATE

ELA	Write a letter to the citizens of Harvestville, convincing them to choose your prototype for the festival. Include linking words (e.g., *since*, *for example*, *as a result*) to connect your opinion to supporting reasons.
ARTS	Create a flyer for the upcoming fall festival, highlighting the newest attraction (your catapult). Remember to give your catapult a unique name.

PROTECT YOURSELF

2-3 HOURS
TIME FOR COMPLETION

s T E A m

SETTING
—THE—
STAGE

DESIGN CHALLENGE PURPOSE

Design and construct a helmet prototype to protect a football player's head.

TEACHER DEVELOPMENT

The lesson requires students to apply the steps of the engineering design process to complete the challenge. Refer to the STEAM Design Process diagram (page 15) for a simple description of each step.

Students will investigate the impact on the skull and brain of athletes who play contact sports, such as American football. Recent revelations about the long-term effects of repeated hits to football players' heads show that, without proper protection, the brain can sustain injury that may not always be recognized at the time of impact.

STUDENT DEVELOPMENT

Students will design and construct a helmet prototype to show the importance of protecting the brain during an impact. The students will need to know the vocabulary associated with the concept of force and motion.

Force is the energy that is applied to an object. **Motion** is the change of position of an object due to a force being applied to the object.

Note: Visit the website listed on the inside front cover for additional resources related to force and motion.

STANDARDS

SCIENCE	TECHNOLOGY	ENGINEERING	ARTS	MATH	ELA
	ISTE.3	K-2-ETS1-1	Creating #1		CCSS.ELA-LITERACY.W.2.2
		K-2-ETS1-2			
		K-2-ETS1-3			

SCIENCE & ENGINEERING PRACTICES

Asking Questions and Defining Problems: Define a simple problem that can be solved through the development of a new or improved object or tool.

CROSSCUTTING CONCEPTS

Structure and Function: The shape and stability of structures of natural and designed objects are related to their function(s).

TARGET VOCABULARY

energy

force

push

MATERIALS

- hard-boiled egg
- 1 sq. ft. of bubble wrap
- tape
- newspaper
- felt
- cotton balls
- egg carton cups

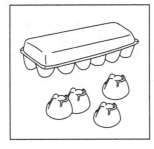

LITERACY CONNECTIONS

Officer Buckle and Gloria
by Peggy Rathmann

NOTES

DILEMMA ENGAGE

Coach Linebacker is the owner of the local sports league in Sportstown. The kids in the league come out on Saturdays to play different sports and get exercise. The past few weeks, the children playing football have reported having headaches after the games. The children explained that they think they need better helmets to protect their heads when they are playing. Coach Linebacker wants to make sure all the students are safe, so he is looking to you to help him design a prototype for a helmet that will protect the children's brains and prevent head injuries.

MISSION

Design and construct a helmet prototype that will protect the model brain (egg) from injury during an impact.

BLUEPRINT EXPLORE

Provide the Individual and Group Blueprint Design Sheets to engineering teams. Have individual students sketch a prototype to present to the other members of their team. Teams will discuss the pros and cons of each sketch and then select one prototype to construct.

ENGINEERING TASK **TEST TRIAL** **ANALYZE** **REDESIGN**

Each engineering team will design and construct a helmet prototype to protect the brain (egg)during an impact.

The teacher will throw all team prototypes against a wall from a distance of 15 ft.

After a helmet prototype has hit the wall, the engineering team will unwrap it to determine if the "skull" remained intact during impact.

Teams should be allowed to observe the other designs to gather ideas, reflect, and make changes in order to improve their prototypes.

Teams can use a colored pencil to make adjustments to their original design sketches. Then they can get new supplies if needed to rebuild and retest their prototypes.

 # HELPFUL TIPS

- After the Test Trial, have teams take a gallery walk to view other teams' designs for possible ideas to assist them in the Analyze and Redesign portions of the engineering design process.

- If teams are successful on the first try, encourage them to make their prototypes even more efficient. If it is a scenario in which this is not feasible, distribute team members to other teams to be a support for them in making their prototypes more efficient. Alternatively, at teacher discretion, move students on to the Justification portion of the lesson.

- If after the third test the final prototype is still unsuccessful, have students write how they would start over. These challenges are meant to have students build on what they originally designed. If the design proved to be unsuccessful, encourage a reflection or justification on what they would do if they were allowed to start again from scratch.

PROTECT YOURSELF

STEAm

REFLECTIONS — EXPLAIN & ELABORATE

AFTER TEST TRIAL 1	Did your prototype protect the "brain"? What materials helped make the helmet prototype succesful?
ANALYSIS	What changes will you make to improve your prototype?
AFTER TEST TRIAL 2	Did the changes you made to your prototype better protect the "brain?"
ANALYSIS	What changes will you make to improve your prototype?
AFTER TEST TRIAL 3	Was your prototype successful? What were some of the similarities and differences between the prototypes?

JUSTIFICATION — EVALUATE

TECHNOLOGY	Use electronic resources to research why helmets and other safety equipment is used in the game of football.
ELA	Write an explanation of how you built and tested your prototype. Include the evidence you collected as you tested it.
ARTS	Create a poster to promote your new helmet design.

SNOW FORT STRUCTURES

STEAM

2-3 HOURS

TIME FOR COMPLETION

SETTING —THE— **STAGE**

DESIGN CHALLENGE PURPOSE

Create the tallest freestanding structure that can support a load.

TEACHER DEVELOPMENT

A **structure** is an object, such as a building, tower, or bridge, that is constructed. The word *structure* can also refer to the way something is built, arranged, or organized. Structures can be built in a variety of ways. Structures are built to support a given load. Certain shapes and designs are stronger than others.

In this lesson, students should be prompted to think about the different shapes and designs of buildings and bridges, as well as the purpose of those shapes in the design of the structure. For example, beam bridges are constructed of straight wood and metal beams. To allow these bridges to span greater distances, shapes such as triangles and squares are added underneath for additional support. Suspension bridges are very flexible, and this enables them to span great distances. Arch bridges are very wide and require more support at the base. Students will need to make connections to the challenge and the challenge materials as they design their prototypes.

SNOW FORT STRUCTURES

STUDENT DEVELOPMENT

This lesson will focus on the purpose and function of structures. Students will need to have an understanding of the importance of structures being able to support weight or loads. It will also be helpful to review two dimensional shapes with students and discuss how they can be arranged in designing their prototypes. Encourage students to discuss with their teams which shapes might be more effective and why before designing.

Lesson Idea: Give groups of students a bag of tangrams or other 2D shapes. Have them sort these shapes based on their characteristics. Then have students play a game of *Who Am I?* Students will give each other clues about a 2D shape based on its attributes. For example, a clue for a triangle might be *I am a three-sided shape. Who am I?*

STANDARDS

SCIENCE	TECHNOLOGY	ENGINEERING	ARTS	MATH	ELA
2-PS1-2	ISTE.1	K-2-ETS1-1	Creating #1	CCSS.MATH.CONTENT.2.MD.A.1	CCSS.ELA-LITERACY.SL.2.1
		K-2-ETS1-2	Creating #2	CCSS.MATH.CONTENT.2.G.A.1	CCSS.ELA-LITERACY.W.2.3
		K-2-ETS1-3	Creating #3		

SCIENCE & ENGINEERING PRACTICES

Developing and Using Models: Develop a simple model based on evidence to represent a proposed object or tool.

Analyzing and Interpreting Data: Analyze data from tests of an object or tool to determine if it works as intended.

CROSSCUTTING CONCEPTS

Structure and Function: The shape and stability of structures of natural and designed objects are related to their function(s).

TARGET VOCABULARY

blueprint

design

load

prototype

structure

support

MATERIALS

Structure:

- 40 toothpicks
- 20 mini marshmallows

Load:

- blocks
- books
- other objects that will be supported by the final prototype

LITERACY CONNECTIONS

Look at That Building!: A First Book of Structures by Scot Ritchie

The Greedy Triangle by Marilyn Burns

NOTES

STEAM

STEAM
— IN —
ACTION

DILEMMA ENGAGE

You and your neighborhood friends just woke up to the best news—it's a snow day! Last night's snowstorm dumped 14 in. of snow on the ground, canceling school for the day. It is the perfect time for a snowball fight! As you know, the first thing your team needs is a sturdy snow fort for protection. The fort needs to be tall enough and wide enough to fit your four team members and also needs to support the weight of your snowballs. It's time to build!

MISSION

Design and build a snow fort that stands the tallest and supports the most weight.

BLUEPRINT EXPLORE

Provide the Individual and Group Blueprint Design Sheets to engineering teams. Have individual students sketch a prototype to present to the other members of their team. Teams will discuss the pros and cons of each sketch and then select one prototype to construct.

ENGINEERING TASK   **TEST TRIAL**   **ANALYZE**   **REDESIGN**

ENGINEERING TASK	TEST TRIAL	ANALYZE	REDESIGN
Engineering teams compete to construct the tallest freestanding fort that can support a load.	Each team will first measure and record the height of its fort. The team will then test the fort by adding a designated load to the structure. If the fort is able to hold the load, additional loads may be added. *Note:* Use the same load to test each team's prototype.	Facilitate analytical discussions comparing the different structures, and designs. Allow teams to reflect on their design compared to other prototypes and what they would do differently. Teams should be allowed to observe the other designs to gather ideas, reflect, and make changes in order to improve their prototypes.	Teams can use a colored pencil to make adjustments to their original design sketches. Then they can get new supplies if needed to rebuild and retest their prototypes.

HELPFUL TIPS

- After the Test Trial, have teams take a gallery walk to view other teams' designs for possible ideas to assist them in the Analyze and Redesign portions of the engineering design process.

- If teams are successful on the first try, encourage them to make their prototypes even more efficient. If it is a scenario in which this is not feasible, distribute team members to other teams to be a support for them in making their prototypes more efficient. Alternatively, at teacher discretion, move students on to the Justification portion of the lesson.

- If after the third test the final prototype is still unsuccessful, have students write how they would start over. These challenges are meant to have students build on what they originally designed. If the design proved to be unsuccessful, encourage a reflection or justification on what they would do if they were allowed to start again from scratch.

STEAM

REFLECTIONS — EXPLAIN & ELABORATE

AFTER TEST TRIAL 1	What was the height of your fort? What were the differences between the prototype with the strongest structure and the other prototypes?
ANALYSIS	What changes did you make to your prototype and why? How did you use what you know about structures to improve your prototype? Did the shape of your design affect the outcome?
AFTER TEST TRIAL 2	Which team of engineers had the most effective prototype? What were the differences between the prototype with the strongest structure and the other prototypes? Which shapes were most effective?
ANALYSIS	What changes did you make to your prototype and why? How did you use what you know about structures to improve your prototype?
AFTER TEST TRIAL 3	What was the final height of your structure? Which team of engineers had the most effective prototype? What were the differences between the prototype with the tallest and strongest structure and the other prototypes?

JUSTIFICATION — EVALUATE

SCIENCE	What materials would you use if you could repeat this challenge? Try completing the challenge with large marshmallows to see if the outcome is the same as the outcome from the original challenge.
TECHNOLOGY/ ARTS	Use a camera to take and print photos of your snow fort prototype. Use the photos and pictures from magazines to illustrate a story about a snowball fight. Include details about your snow fort.
ELA	Write narratives in which you recount the events that took place on your snow day. Include details to describe actions, thoughts, and feelings. Use temporal words and phrases (e.g., *first, eventually, finally*) to signal event order and provide a sense of closure.

TROLL TRANSPORT

1 HOUR

TIME FOR COMPLETION

SETTING —THE— STAGE

DESIGN CHALLENGE PURPOSE

Create a wind-powered vehicle that can travel on water.

TEACHER DEVELOPMENT

The lesson requires students to apply the steps of the engineering design process to complete the challenge. Refer to the diagram of the STEAM design process (page 15) for a description of each step.

Students will also need to understand the concept of **buoyancy**. Buoyancy is an object's ability to float in water, air, or another fluid. An object's ability to sink or float is a property of matter. This challenge focuses on creating a structure that floats and is able to move across the water when powered by wind.

STUDENT DEVELOPMENT

This is a great lesson for teaching the engineering process to students. Introduce the words **blueprint**, **design**, **engineer**, and **prototype** to your students. Teach them how to collaborate and work as a team. Use the STEAM Job Cards (page 145) to assign jobs to students to demonstrate the importance of working together.

Lesson Idea: Sink or Float? Have students use a variety of objects to predict whether an object will sink or float when placed in a container of water. Place objects in a tub of water one at a time. Have students observe what happens and record the results in a science notebook. Discuss the characteristics of the objects that floated.

STANDARDS

SCIENCE	TECHNOLOGY	ENGINEERING	ARTS	MATH	ELA
		K-2-ETS1-1	Creating #1	CCSS.MATH. CONTENT.2.MD.A.1	CCSS.ELA-LITERACY.W.2.3
		K-2-ETS1-2	Creating #2		
		K-2-ETS1-3	Creating #3		
			Presenting #6		

SCIENCE & ENGINEERING PRACTICES

Asking Questions and Defining Problems: Ask questions based on observations to find more information about the natural and/or designed world.

Define a simple problem that can be solved through the development of a new or improved object or tool.

Developing and Using Models: Develop a simple model based on evidence to represent a proposed object or tool.

Analyzing and Interpreting Data: Analyze data from tests of an object or tool to determine if it works as intended.

CROSSCUTTING CONCEPTS

Structure and Function: The shape and stability of structures of natural and designed objects are related to their function(s).

TARGET VOCABULARY

blueprint

buoyancy

design

engineer

float

prototype

wind-powered

MATERIALS

- 5 straws (4 for construction, 1 for simulating wind)
- 1 large marshmallow
- ruler
- scissors
- tape
- tub of water
- 2 twist ties
- 2 rubberbands

Teams select one of the following materials for the prototype:

- 1 sheet tissue paper
- 1 sheet wax paper
- 1 sheet construction paper

Note: Students may cut their "wind" straw into multiple pieces to allow more than one person to simulate wind.

LITERACY CONNECTIONS

The Three Billy Goats Gruff by Paul Galdone

NOTES

STEAM
— IN —
ACTION

DILEMMA ENGAGE

My name is Trevor and I need your help! If you've read the story of "The Three Billy Goats Gruff," you may have heard of me. I'm the troll. Those goats tricked me quite unfairly. That last one knocked me right into the river. Maybe you think I deserved it, but that's where you're wrong. My whole purpose in life is to guard my bridge. They didn't have to trip, trap across it, did they? Now I'm in terrible trouble. I'm stuck on a rock in the middle of the river, and I need to get back to my bridge. If you are wondering why I don't just swim back to my bridge or swim to shore, I can assure you I have a very good reason. It's rather embarrassing… trolls can't swim! I've just been sitting on this rock with my blanket and a few sticks that I've collected as they've drifted by on the current. I need to build something that will carry me back to my bridge. Can you help me build a model of a transportation device that will keep me dry and help me get back to my bridge? Please hurry! It's very windy out here in the middle of this river.

MISSION

Build a model of a transportation device that will travel across the water using only wind power. Place a marshmallow on the boat to represent Trevor. Remember, he can't swim so your marshmallow can't get wet!

BLUEPRINT EXPLORE

Provide the Individual and Group Blueprint Design Sheets to engineering teams. Have individual students sketch a prototype to present to the other members of their team. Teams will discuss the pros and cons of each sketch and then select one prototype to construct.

Note: It is essential that students use measurements in their plan and when they are building their actual prototype.

ENGINEERING TASK　　 **TEST TRIAL**　　 **ANALYZE**　　 **REDESIGN**

ENGINEERING TASK	TEST TRIAL	ANALYZE	REDESIGN
Each team will create a prototype that floats, uses wind to move across the water, and keeps the marshmallow on it dry. *Note:* In order to meet the math standard, teams must be held to the measurements in their design when building their prototypes.	Each team will place its prototype in the water against one side of the container. The team will place the marshmallow on the prototype and then blow through a straw to simulate wind. Team members will try to move their boats to the opposite side of the container.	Facilitate analytical discussions comparing the structures and designs of the prototypes. Allow teams to reflect on their designs compared to others and what they would do differently. Teams should be allowed to observe the other designs to gather ideas, reflect, and make changes in order to improve their prototypes.	Teams can use a colored pencil to make adjustments to their original design sketches. Then they can get new supplies if needed to rebuild and retest their prototypes.

HELPFUL TIPS

- After the Test Trial, have teams take a gallery walk to view other teams' designs for possible ideas to assist them in the Analyze and Redesign portions of the engineering design process.

- If teams are successful on the first try, encourage them to make their prototypes even more efficient. If it is a scenario in which this is not feasible, distribute team members to other teams to be a support for them in making their prototypes more efficient. Alternatively, at teacher discretion, move students on to the Justification portion of the lesson.

- If after the third test the final prototype is still unsuccessful, have students write how they would start over. These challenges are meant to have students build on what they originally designed. If the design proved to be unsuccessful, encourage a reflection or justification on what they would do if they were allowed to start again from scratch.

sTEAM

REFLECTIONS — EXPLAIN & ELABORATE

AFTER TEST TRIAL 1	Which teams were able to transport their troll across the river without it falling into the water? What material did those teams use for their sails?
ANALYSIS	What changes will you make to your prototype?
AFTER TEST TRIAL 2	Which team had the safest troll transportation device? Which teams were able to get their troll transports across the river?
ANALYSIS	What will you do differently to improve your troll transportation device?
AFTER TEST TRIAL 3	How did your team's troll transportation device compare to the other teams' prototypes?

JUSTIFICATION — EVALUATE

ELA	Write a story from the point of view of the troll from "The Three Billy Goats Gruff."
ARTS	Draw a cover for your story that clearly shows the point of view of the troll, rather than that of the goats.

BE A BEE!

S T E A m

SETTING —THE— STAGE

DESIGN CHALLENGE PURPOSE

Create a model that represents how bees pollinate plants.

TEACHER DEVELOPMENT

Pollination is part of the plant reproduction process. Pollen is produced in the male part (the **anthers**) of the flowering plant. It then needs to be transferred to the female part (the **stigma**) of the flower or of a flower of the same species. Fertilization occurs and seeds are produced.

How do bees pollinate? Bees have small hairs that get a static electric charge as they fly through the air. This charge collects the pollen when they land on a flower. Then when they go to another flower, there is a discharge of electricity that releases the pollen onto the new flower.

Static electricity is taught more in depth in third grade. However, since this is one way bees transfer pollen, a brief introduction to the concept is appropriate. All matter is made up of atoms. **Atoms** contain protons,

neutrons, and electrons. Electrons are negatively charged. When objects rub against each other, electrons can move from one object to another. **Static electricity** is when an object collects an excess number of negatively charged electrons. Objects that have opposite charges are attracted to each other, like when you brush your hair and it becomes attracted to the comb and stands up all over.

In September of 2016, an area was sprayed for mosquitos and it ended up killing millions of bees in South Carolina. This was devastating to the area because bees are already an endangered species. Bees pollinate the plants that grow most of the fruits and vegetables we eat.

Visit the website listed on the inside front cover for more information about the endangered honeybee.

STUDENT DEVELOPMENT

Review pollination with your students and give a brief overview of the concept of static electricity in relation to the attraction of negatively charged objects to positively charged objects.

Lesson Idea: Glue a paper flower onto the side of a paper cup. Fill the cup with cheese puffs. Glue another paper flower onto another cup. Have students grab and eat the cheese puffs from the first cup. Students should not clean off their hands! Have them touch the paper flower on the empty cup. Have students discuss what they observed when they took the cheese puffs and when they touched the empty cup.

To introduce static electricity to the class, have students rub a balloon on their shirts, against their hair, or with a wool cloth. Have students hold the charged balloon close to their arms to observe what happens to the hairs on their arms.

STANDARDS

SCIENCE	TECHNOLOGY	ENGINEERING	ARTS	MATH	ELA
2-LS2-2	ISTE.3	K-2-ETS1-1	Creating #1		CCSS.ELA-LITERACY.W.2.1
	ISTE.4	K-2-ETS1-2	Creating #2		
		K-2-ETS1-3	Creating #3		

SCIENCE & ENGINEERING PRACTICES

Developing and Using Models: Develop a simple model based on evidence to represent a proposed object or tool.

CROSSCUTTING CONCEPTS

Structure and Function: The shape and stability of structures of natural and designed objects are related to their function(s).

TARGET VOCABULARY

bee

pollen

pollinate

static electricity

MATERIALS

Flowers:

- 2 silk or plastic flowers
- 20 pieces of paper confetti

Tools:

- pipe cleaners
- cotton balls
- small balloons
- craft sticks
- felt
- tissue paper

LITERACY CONNECTIONS

What If There Were No Bees?
by Suzanne Slade

NOTES

DILEMMA ENGAGE

The farming community in Dorchester County, South Carolina, is in a panic. The annual Dorchester Pumpkin Festival is coming soon, and there may not be any pumpkins. In an attempt to kill mosquitos and protect people from the Zika virus, a poison was sprayed with a terrible result—millions of bees were also killed. Bees are responsible for the pollination of all the pumpkin plants in the area. While farmers are saddened by this tragedy, they are now worried about not having any pumpkins for the annual pumpkin festival. The festival brings much needed money and attention to the town. The farmers need your help!

MISSION

Build a tool that uses static electricity to simulate the pollination of flowers, just like the bees use static electricity to move pollen from one flower to another.

BLUEPRINT EXPLORE

Provide the Individual and Group Blueprint Design Sheets to engineering teams. Have individual students sketch a prototype to present to the other members of their team. Teams will discuss the pros and cons of each sketch and then select one prototype to construct.

ENGINEERING TASK **TEST TRIAL** **ANALYZE** **REDESIGN**

ENGINEERING TASK	TEST TRIAL	ANALYZE	REDESIGN
Each team will create a tool that collects "pollen" using static electricity.	Each team will use its tool to transfer "pollen" (confetti pieces) from one flower to another. Students may not use their hands to hold or touch the flowers. They may only touch the tool. For each test, teams may only touch the flowers with their tool one time. Teams may rub the tool on their clothes or with a wool cloth to build up static electricty prior to the test.	Teams will count the number of confetti pieces they were able to successfully transfer from one flower to another using their tool. Teams should be allowed to observe the other designs to gather ideas, reflect, and make changes in order to improve their prototypes.	Teams can use a colored pencil to make adjustments to their original design sketches. Then they can get new supplies if needed to rebuild and retest their prototypes.

 HELPFUL TIPS

- After the Test Trial, have teams take a gallery walk to view other teams' designs for possible ideas to assist them in the Analyze and Redesign portions of the engineering design process.

- If teams are successful on the first try, encourage them to make their prototypes even more efficient. If it is a scenario in which this is not feasible, distribute team members to other teams to be a support for them in making their prototypes more efficient. Alternatively, at teacher discretion, move students on to the Justification portion of the lesson.

- If after the third test the final prototype is still unsuccessful, have students write how they would start over. These challenges are meant to have students build on what they originally designed. If the design proved to be unsuccessful, encourage a reflection or justification on what they would do if they were allowed to start again from scratch.

REFLECTIONS — EXPLAIN & ELABORATE

AFTER TEST TRIAL 1	How many "pollen" pieces were you able to transfer from one flower to another using your tool? Which team transferred the most "pollen"? What are some differences between the most successful prototype and the prototypes used by the other teams?
ANALYSIS	What will your team change about your prototype in order to collect more "pollen" and successfully transfer it to the second flower?
AFTER TEST TRIAL 2	Did the amount of "pollen" you collected from the first flower increase? Explain. Was your team able to successfully transfer all of the "pollen" you picked up from the first flower to the second? Explain.
ANALYSIS	What will you change about your prototype in order to increase the amount of "pollen" collected and successfully transferred from one flower to another?
AFTER TEST TRIAL 3	Did the changes your team made to your prototype increase the amount of "pollen" successfully transferred from one flower to another?

JUSTIFICATION — EVALUATE

TECHNOLOGY	Use the Internet to research honeybees to find out why they are considered an endangered species and what the public can do to help.
ELA	*Note:* Students will need a copy of the newspaper outline on page 132. Write a newspaper article explaining why honeybees are endangered. Include ways that humans can help protect them.
ARTS	Create a model of a bee using clay and other art materials.

BUILD A ZOO

3-4 HOURS

TIME FOR COMPLETION

S t e A m

SETTING —THE— STAGE

DESIGN CHALLENGE PURPOSE

Create a realistic diorama depicting a specific habitat.

TEACHER DEVELOPMENT

This lesson focuses on the science standard 2-LS4-1. This standard requires students to make observations of plants and animals to compare the diversity of life in different habitats. The arts standards are focused on both the creating and the presentation pieces of this challenge. Students must be prepared to present their design to an audience, so some guidelines and expectations will need to be set prior to starting this lesson. Review the rubric (page 133) with students before the lesson.

STUDENT DEVELOPMENT

Each group will be assigned a different habitat. In order for students to make observations for this lesson, habitat WebQuests, websites, and texts must be provided for group research and recording. Provide some time to complete parts of habitat WebQuests with the whole group. Have students complete the Habitat Research Outline (page 134) in order to record information about animals and plants from their habitat as well as any other interesting information they think may help make their model more realistic.

Note: Visit the website listed on the inside front cover for more information about habitats.

STANDARDS

SCIENCE	TECHNOLOGY	ENGINEERING	ARTS	MATH	ELA
2-LS4-1			Creating #1		CCSS.ELA-LITERACY.SL.2.1
			Creating #2		CCSS.ELA-LITERACY.W.2.3
			Creating #3		CCSS.ELA-LITERACY.W.2.7
			Performing/Presenting/Producing #4, #5, #6		CCSS.ELA-LITERACY.W.2.8

SCIENCE & ENGINEERING PRACTICES

Planning and Carrying Out Investigations: Make observations (firsthand or from media) to collect data that can be used to make comparisons.

Scientific Knowledge Is Based on Empirical Evidence: Scientists look for patterns and order when making observations about the world.

CROSSCUTTING CONCEPTS

Patterns: Patterns in the natural and human-designed world can be observed.

TARGET VOCABULARY

diversity

habitat

observation

MATERIALS

- shoebox
- empty cereal box
- modeling clay
- construction paper
- glue
- tape
- paint
- cotton balls
- sand
- pebbles
- plastic wrap
- aluminum foil
- newspaper
- magazines
- other materials students bring from home
- zoo rubric (page 133)
- habitat outline (page 134)

LITERACY CONNECTIONS

I See a Kookaburra! Discovering Animal Habitats Around the World
by Steve Jenkins and Robin Page

National Geographic Little Kids First Big Book of Animals
by Catherine D. Hughes

NOTES

S t e A m

STEAM
—IN—
ACTION

DILEMMA ENGAGE

Mrs. Ann E. Mull, the mayor of Divercity, has just made a special announcement to all citizens. Divercity is getting ready to open its very first zoo, and the mayor is asking for your help in the design process! Mrs. Mull wants to create a zoo full of a variety of plants and animals to attract visitors from across the globe. In order to ensure that all habitats are included, she needs help in designing each of the six unique areas of the zoo. The zoo will need to include animals and plants from the grassland, rain forest, desert, polar regions, ocean, and temperate forest.

MISSION

Design and construct a model (diorama) of a habitat. Include at least four different plants and four different animals that are native to that area. Present your final diorama to an audience.

BLUEPRINT EXPLORE

Provide the Individual and Group Blueprint Design Sheets to engineering teams. Have individual students sketch a prototype to present to the other members of their team. Teams will discuss the pros and cons of each sketch and then select one prototype to construct.

ENGINEERING TASK TEST TRIAL ANALYZE REDESIGN

ENGINEERING TASK	TEST TRIAL	ANALYZE	REDESIGN
Each team will construct a realistic habitat diorama and present it to an audience. *Note*: The teacher completes the Build A Zoo Rubric as each team presents its model to the class.	Each team will present its diorama to another team. These two teams will take turns presenting to each other. Have teams write feedback about each other's presentation and diorama using sticky notes, half sheets of paper, or index cards. Remind teams to say something they like about the other team's diorama along with one suggestion for improvement.	Facilitate analytical discussions comparing the different designs. Allow teams to reflect on their dioramas compared to others and what they would do differently. Teams should be allowed to observe the other designs to gather ideas, reflect, and make changes in order to improve their prototypes.	Teams can use a colored pencil to make adjustments to their original design sketches. Then they can get new supplies if needed to rebuild and retest their prototypes.

HELPFUL TIPS

- After the Test Trial, have teams take a gallery walk to view other teams' designs for possible ideas to assist them in the Analyze and Redesign portions of the engineering design process.

- Repeat the procedure suggested in test trial for the second test trial, this time pairing up different teams.

- Teams will present their dioramas to the entire class and answer questions from the audience during the third test trial.

- Teachers may decide to have only one test trial prior to teams presenting to the class. However, three test trials give students more practice presenting in front of an audience and gives them more exposure to the content.

REFLECTIONS — EXPLAIN & ELABORATE

AFTER TEST TRIAL 1	Did your model include at least four plants and four animals?
ANALYSIS	What parts of your habitat would tell the audience what habitat it represents? What additional items can you add to your model so it resembles the habitat you were assigned?
AFTER TEST TRIAL 2	Did your model include at least four different plant and four different animal species? Did your team work well together in making decisions and carrying out changes to improve your model?
ANALYSIS	What parts of your habitat would tell the audience what habitat it represents? What additional items can you add to your model so it resembles the habitat you were assigned?
AFTER TEST TRIAL 3	Were you able to make your model more realistic this time around? What changes did you make and why?

JUSTIFICATION — EVALUATE

ELA	*Note:* Students will need a copy of the A Day in the Life Of reproducible on page 135. Write a story that tells about a day in the life of an animal from your habitat. Include details to describe actions, thoughts, and feelings. Use temporal words and phrases, such as *at first*, *before*, and *eventually*, to signal event order and provide a sense of closure.
ARTS	Design and illustrate a brochure outlining important information about the plants and animals represented in your habitat model.

GROW, PLANT, GROW!

10 HOURS

TIME FOR COMPLETION

SPREAD OVER 10 - 14 DAYS

SETTING —THE— STAGE

DESIGN CHALLENGE PURPOSE

Observe the differences between the growth of plants that receive sunlight and plants that do not.

TEACHER DEVELOPMENT

Plants need sunlight and water to grow. Plants come from seeds, which sprout into **seedlings** when they receive the sunlight and water they need. **Seeds** are protected by a seed coat on the outside. Inside the seeds is the **embryo** (baby plant) and food storage that the plant first uses to sprout from seed to seedling, or small plant. The science standard for second grade says that students plan and conduct an investigation about the growth of plants that is limited to testing one variable at a time. Since this activity is testing a plant's ability to grow without sunlight, it is important to remind students that all other variables must be the same.

Note: This challenge should be done at a time of year when you will have a fairly consistent amount of sun each day. If you do not have enough space for the plants inside a closet or cupboard, put the plants under old shoeboxes.

STUDENT DEVELOPMENT

Review the life cycle of a plant beginning with it sprouting from a seed. A **seed** germinates when it receives enough sunlight and water. It is during this germination process that the plant sprouts from the seed. We call this sprout a **seedling**. With the right amount of sunlight, water, and nutrients from the soil, the seedling will grow into an adult plant. Eventually, the adult plant will reproduce by forming new seeds, which continues the cycle.

Lesson Idea: Soak 25 lima bean seeds in water overnight. The next day, give each pair of students two seeds and two toothpicks. Have students carefully break open the seed. Inside, they will see the part of the plant that will become a seedling. This is called the **embryo**.

STANDARDS

SCIENCE	TECHNOLOGY	ENGINEERING	ARTS	MATH	ELA
2-LS2-1	ISTE.3		Creating #1	CCSS.MATH.CONTENT.2.MD.A.1	CCSS.ELA-LITERACY.W.2.8
			Creating #2		
			Creating #3		

SCIENCE & ENGINEERING PRACTICES

Planning and Carrying out Investigations: Plan and conduct an investigation collaboratively to produce data to serve as the basis for evidence to answer a question.

Make observations (firsthand or from media) to collect data that can be used to make comparisons.

CROSSCUTTING CONCEPTS

Cause and Effect: Events have causes that generate observable patterns.

TARGET VOCABULARY

embryo

plant

seed

seedling

variable

MATERIALS

- 6 lima bean seeds
- 6 cups or pots
- soil
- water
- marker
- ruler

LITERACY CONNECTIONS

The Empty Pot
by Demi

NOTES

STEAM Design Challenges Gr. 2 © 2017 Creative Teaching Press

DILEMMA — ENGAGE

The emperor has given you a plot of land to grow food for the villagers, but he has forbidden you to take down the gazebos that shade much of the area. He has given you a packet of lima bean seeds to begin your crop. You want to grow as many plants as possible, but you don't want to waste the precious seeds or disappoint the emperor. You are not sure if seeds planted under the gazebos will grow. You decide to conduct a test with just six lima bean seeds before planting them all.

Note: If you are not using the suggested literacy connection, *The Empty Pot* by Demi, adjust the dilemma by changing *emperor* to *parents* and *the villagers* to *family*.

MISSION

Plant six lima beans in soil. Observe what happens when three seeds receive sunlight and three seeds receive none. All six plants will receive 10 ml of water every other day.

BLUEPRINT — EXPLORE

Create a plant journal: Have students fold five sheets of blank paper in half. Teachers should staple along the folded edge to create the journal for student observations. Students will use this journal to record their observations and answer the reflection questions.

ENGINEERING TASK	TEST TRIAL	ANALYZE	REDESIGN
Observation set up: Each team plants its six seeds each in their own cup or pot filled with soil. Each cup should be numbered 1–6. The team should give each plant 10 ml of water and then set up the cups for observation. Three of the plants should be placed in a sunny area, while the other three should be placed in a dark closet or cabinet.	Observe all six plants every other day for approximately 10 to 14 days. Measure any plant growth and record observations in your plant journal.	In your plant journal, record your observations of any plant growth. Write statements that compare and contrast the results of the two groups of plants.	This is not applicable to this challenge.

HELPFUL TIPS

- After the Test Trial, have teams take a gallery walk to view other teams' designs for possible ideas to assist them in the Analyze and Redesign portions of the engineering design process.

- If teams are successful on the first try, encourage them to make their prototypes even more efficient. If it is a scenario in which this is not feasible, distribute team members to other teams to be a support for them in making their prototypes more efficient. Alternatively, at teacher discretion, move students on to the Justification portion of the lesson.

- If after the third test the final prototype is still unsuccessful, have students write how they would start over. These challenges are meant to have students build on what they originally designed. If the design proved to be unsuccessful, encourage a reflection or justification on what they would do if they were allowed to start again from scratch.

REFLECTIONS — EXPLAIN & ELABORATE

AFTER TEST TRIAL 1	After the fourth day of observations, what did you notice about the plants in the sunlight? What did you notice about the plants in the dark? What was the height of the tallest plant? Which group did it belong to (light or no light)?
ANALYSIS	What conclusions can you draw from your observations so far?
AFTER TEST TRIAL 2	After the eighth day of observations, what are the similarities and/or differences between the two groups (light and no light)? Explain. What is the height of the tallest plant? Which group does it belong to? What is the height of the shortest plant? What group does it belong to?
ANALYSIS	From your observations so far, what conclusions can you make about the two groups of plants?
AFTER TEST TRIAL 3	Record your final observations, along with the heights of the plants in each group. What conclusion can you make based on your results?

JUSTIFICATION — EVALUATE

TECHNOLOGY	Complete a WebQuest or use an interactive website to research facts about a specific plant species. Include information about the life cycle of the plant. Organize this information using index cards or in a science notebook. Visit the website listed on the inside front cover for more information about WebQuests.
ELA	Write a report about what you learned from the plant observations.
ARTS	Use the Grow, Plant, Grow! plant markers (page 136) to create garden markers for your favorite vegetables. Include both an illustration and the name of the vegetable. Attach completed plant markers to craft sticks and place in the garden.

SPREAD THE SEEDS

sTEAM

SETTING —THE— STAGE

DESIGN CHALLENGE PURPOSE

Design a new insect that will be able to transport seeds.

TEACHER DEVELOPMENT

This challenge focuses on how animals play a role in the life cycle of some plants by helping to **transport** seeds from one place to another. In order for students to complete this challenge, they will first need to research the ways different animals move seeds from one place to another. One example of the role an animal plays in a plant's life cycle is when a monkey eats a piece of fruit and releases the fruit's seeds in its waste material.

Note: Visit the website listed on the inside front cover for more information about animals and how they help transport seeds from one place to another.

SPREAD THE SEEDS

STUDENT DEVELOPMENT

To provide students with necessary background information they will need for this challenge, engineering teams must first complete an animal WebQuest or conduct research using the provided websites and texts. Have teams complete the Animal Research Outline (page 137) as they conduct their research, recording information they think may help make their prototype more realistic.

STANDARDS

SCIENCE	TECHNOLOGY	ENGINEERING	ARTS	MATH	ELA
2-LS2-2		K-2-ETS1-1	Creating #1		CCSS.ELA-LITERACY.RI.2.3
		K-2-ETS1-2	Creating #2		CCSS.ELA-LITERACY.W.2.3
			Creating #3		CCSS.ELA-LITERACY.W.2.7
					CCSS.ELA-LITERACY.W.2.8

SCIENCE & ENGINEERING PRACTICES

Developing and Using Models: Develop a simple model based on evidence to represent a proposed object or tool.

STEAM Design Challenges Gr. 2 © 2017 Creative Teaching Press

93

CROSSCUTTING CONCEPTS

Structure and Function: The shape and stability of structures of natural and designed objects are related to their function.

TARGET VOCABULARY

seed

transport

MATERIALS

- colored pencils
- modeling clay
- small paper cups
- string
- pipe cleaners
- straws
- construction paper
- paper
- pencil
- research outline (page 137)
- prototype rubric (page 138)

LITERACY CONNECTIONS

The Dandelion Seed by Joseph Anthony

A Fruit Is a Suitcase for Seeds by Jean Richards

NOTES

STEAM —IN— ACTION

DILEMMA ENGAGE

In the land of Blumeria, the animals were responsible for transporting seeds from one plant to another. Last summer, Blumeria was destroyed by a hurricane! Most of the animals left and found a new place to live. They named their new home New Blumeria. The mayor of New Blumeria needs to find animals that can help transport the seeds in the new town. Help the mayor and the citizens of New Blumeria by designing an animal that can help transport seeds.

MISSION

Design an animal that can collect and transport seeds.

BLUEPRINT EXPLORE

Provide the Individual and Group Blueprint Design Sheets to engineering teams. Have individual students sketch a prototype to present to the other members of their team. Teams will discuss the pros and cons of each sketch and then select one prototype to construct.

ENGINEERING TASK	TEST TRIAL	ANALYZE	REDESIGN
Each team will design and build an animal that can collect and transport seeds.	Each team will display its new animal for the teacher to review. The teacher will fill out and return the rubric to teams to help during the redesign process.	Teams will participate in a gallery walk during which they observe the different prototypes to gather ideas and determine which animal would be most effective at transporting seeds.	Teams will use the information on the rubric to redesign and improve their animal prototypes.
		Teams should be allowed to observe the other designs to gather ideas, reflect, and make changes in order to improve their prototypes.	Teams can use a colored pencil to make adjustments to their original design sketches. Then they can get new supplies if needed to rebuild and retest their prototypes.

 # HELPFUL TIPS

- After the Test Trial, have teams take a gallery walk to view other teams' designs for possible ideas to assist them in the Analyze and Redesign portions of the engineering design process.

- If teams are successful on the first try, encourage them to make their prototypes even more efficient. If it is a scenario in which this is not feasible, distribute team members to other teams to be a support for them in making their prototypes more efficient. Alternatively, at teacher discretion, move students on to the Justification portion of the lesson.

- If after the third test the final prototype is still unsuccessful, have students write how they would start over. These challenges are meant to have students build on what they originally designed. If the design proved to be unsuccessful, encourage a reflection or justification on what they would do if they were allowed to start again from scratch.

REFLECTIONS — EXPLAIN & ELABORATE

AFTER TEST TRIAL 1	What feedback did you receive on your rubric for your animal? What changes could you make to your animal to improve your prototype?
ANALYSIS	Which animal characteristics do you feel make your animal most effective in transporting seeds? What characteristics from other teams were different from yours?
AFTER TEST TRIAL 2	What feedback did you receive on your rubric? Did your score improve this time around?
ANALYSIS	Which animal characteristics received the most positive feedback? What could you add to your design to improve your prototype?
AFTER TEST TRIAL 3	What was your team's final score? How did your background knowledge about how animals transport seeds help your team to improve on its design?

JUSTIFICATION — EVALUATE

ELA

Note: Students will need a copy of the A Day in the Life Of reproducible on page 135.

Write a story about your new animal called "A Day in the Life of ___." Explain how your animal collects and transports seeds. Include details to describe actions, thoughts, and feelings. Use temporal words, such as *first*, *next*, and *finally*, to signal event order and provide a sense of closure.

DIRECTIONAL MISHAPS

StEAM

1 HOUR
TIME FOR COMPLETION

SETTING
—THE—
STAGE

DESIGN CHALLENGE PURPOSE

Create an object out of tangrams by following an algorithm.

TEACHER DEVELOPMENT

Algorithms are a list of steps to complete a task. We use algorithms throughout our day, such as when filling out forms, following recipes, and playing a sport. Computers use algorithms too! This challenge will teach students how to create simple algorithms. This skill can be used as a foundation for beginning computer programming. You can either use tangram pieces from your math supplies or cut the shapes out of paper.

Tangrams are thought to have originated during the Tang Dynasty in Imperial China. There are seven known flat shapes (tans): 2 large triangles, 1 medium triangle, 2 small triangles, 1 parallelogram, and 1 square. The following ancient rules are the same ones to follow for this challenge:

- tans must touch
- tans must lay flat
- tans cannot overlap
- tans must combine to create a picture or design

STUDENT DEVELOPMENT

The best way for students to develop a deeper understanding of tangrams is to read books about them and have lots of practice using them to complete tangram activities. Assign each student a partner and have partners work together to use the tangrams to create different animals. Next, have them practice giving clear directions to each other by writing down the directions for a procedure you follow every school day, such as lining up to leave the classroom for recess or preparing to leave the classroom at the end of the day. Have one student from each pair write down the step-by-step directions and give them to his or her partner to check for accuracy.

STANDARDS

SCIENCE	TECHNOLOGY	ENGINEERING	ARTS	MATH	ELA
2-PS1-3		K-2-ETS1-1	Creating #1	CCSS.MATH. CONTENT.2.G.A.1	CCSS.ELA-LITERACY.W.2.3
		K-2-ETS1-2	Creating #2		CCSS.ELA-LITERACY.SL.2.1
		K-2-ETS1-3	Creating #3		

SCIENCE & ENGINEERING PRACTICES

Constructing Explanations and Designing Solutions: Make observations (firsthand or from media) to construct an evidence-based account for natural phenomena.

CROSSCUTTING CONCEPTS

Energy and Matter: Objects may break into smaller pieces and be put together into larger pieces, or change shapes.

TARGET VOCABULARY

algorithm

tangram

MATERIALS

- shoebox (to hide tangram animal)
- paper
- pencil

LITERACY CONNECTIONS

Grandfather Tang's Story
by Ann Tompert

Tangram: 1,600 Ancient Chinese Puzzles
by Joost Elffers

NOTES

STEAM
—IN—
ACTION

DILEMMA ENGAGE

Mrs. In-control has been working with her students on following directions. However, the students are now bored with all of the activities she usually uses. Mrs. In-control needs help! She knows that her students love tangrams and thinks that an activity that uses tangrams might get them excited about practicing their direction-following skills. Help Mrs. In-control by testing a tangram activity before she does the activity with her students.

MISSION

Create a tangram animal. Then write a set of directions for another team to follow to help them recreate the tangram animal.

BLUEPRINT EXPLORE

Provide the Individual and Group Blueprint Design Sheets to engineering teams. Have individual students design and sketch an animal tangram, write the directions for recreating it, and then present it to his or her partner. Engineering teams must discuss the pros and cons of each sketch and then select the tangram animal (with directions) they will use for the challenge.

Note: This activity works best with teams of two students.

ENGINEERING TASK

 TEST TRIAL

 ANALYZE

 REDESIGN

ENGINEERING TASK

Each team will create a tangram animal and write detailed directions for recreating it. Other teams will use the directions provided to attempt to duplicate the animal.

TEST TRIAL

Each team will create its tangram animal, write the directions for creating it, and then hide the animal under a shoebox. The directions for creating the tangram animal should be placed next to the box for other teams to use as they attempt to recreate the animal. Once it is completed, the team lifts off the box to compare its tangrams to the original design. Both tangram animals are left in place (side by side) so the team that created it can analyze the results.

ANALYZE

Was the other team able to follow your directions? If the animals don't look alike, how can you change the directions to get an accurate result?

REDESIGN

Teams will make the necessary changes to their directions to ensure they are clear and easy to undestand.

Ensure that different teams attempt to follow the directions and create an animal tangram for each other so that no team attempts to recreate the same tangram animal twice.

 HELPFUL TIPS

- After the Test Trial, have teams take a gallery walk to view other teams' designs for possible ideas to assist them in the Analyze and Redesign portions of the engineering design process.

- If teams are successful on the first try, encourage them to make their prototypes even more efficient. If it is a scenario in which this is not feasible, distribute team members to other teams to be a support for them in making their prototypes more efficient. Alternatively, at teacher discretion, move students on to the Justification portion of the lesson.

- If after the third test the final prototype is still unsuccessful, have students write how they would start over. These challenges are meant to have students build on what they originally designed. If the design proved to be unsuccessful, encourage a reflection or justification on what they would do if they were allowed to start again from scratch.

STEAM Design Challenges Gr. 2 © 2017 Creative Teaching Press

STEAM

REFLECTIONS — EXPLAIN & ELABORATE

AFTER TEST TRIAL 1	Did the other team succesfully follow your directions? Did its tangram animal match your tangram animal under the box?
ANALYSIS	What part of the directions can you change to make them more clear and easy to understand?
AFTER TEST TRIAL 2	Did your changes help? Do the animals look exactly alike now? What was different? What was the same?
ANALYSIS	How can you improve the directions to make them easy to understand?
AFTER TEST TRIAL 3	Do the two animals match?

JUSTIFICATION — EVALUATE

ELA	Write a narrative about your tangram animal that can be displayed with your tangram.
ARTS	Trace the tangram animal onto a blank piece of paper. Create a habitat for your animal by drawing the habitat or by cutting out paper and gluing it onto the page.

HELP HUMPTY!

2 HOURS

TIME FOR COMPLETION

SETTING —THE— STAGE

DESIGN CHALLENGE PURPOSE

Design and construct a way to keep Humpty safe when he takes a fall.

TEACHER DEVELOPMENT

This challenge focuses on **matter** and its **properties**. Different types of materials can be classified by their observable properties. Examples of properties include **strength**, **flexibility**, **hardness**, **texture**, and **absorbency**. **Flexibility** is the capability of being bent. **Texture** is the way something feels. **Absorbency** is the ability to take in and hold water. These properties should be taken into account and discussed when teams are deciding on materials and their uses for this design challenge.

STUDENT DEVELOPMENT

Before this lesson, students should practice observing and classifying different solids according to their observable properties. Review vocabulary words (i.e., **properties**, **strength**, **flexibility**, **hardness**, **texture**, and **absorbency**) and examples with students.

Lesson Idea: Students participate in a scavenger hunt, looking for items around the classroom. Items should be sorted according to their properties. Students can then play a game of I Spy, completing riddles using the items' properties as clues. For example, one student would say *I spy an object used for measuring the length of other things. It is not flexible and has a smooth texture. What it is?*

STANDARDS

SCIENCE	TECHNOLOGY	ENGINEERING	ARTS	MATH	ELA
2-PS1-1		K-2-ETS1-1	Creating #1		CCSS.ELA-LITERACY.SL.2.1
2-PS1-2		K-2-ETS1-2	Creating #2		CCSS.ELA-LITERACY.W.2.3
2-PS1-3		K-2-ETS1-3	Creating #3		

SCIENCE & ENGINEERING PRACTICES

Planning and Carrying Out Investigations: Plan and conduct an investigation collaboratively to produce data to serve as the basis for evidence to answer a question.

Analyzing and Interpreting Data: Analyze data from tests of an object or tool to determine if it worked as intended.

CROSSCUTTING CONCEPTS

Patterns: Patterns in the natural and human-designed world can be observed.

Cause and Effect: Simple tests can be designed to gather evidence to support or refute student ideas about causes.

Energy and Matter: Objects may break into smaller pieces and be put together into larger pieces, or change shapes.

Influence of Engineering, Technology, and Science on Society and the Natural World: Every human-made product is designed by applying some knowledge of the natural world and is built using materials derived from the natural world.

TARGET VOCABULARY

absorbency

flexibility

hardness

matter

property

strength

texture

MATERIALS

- tape
- newspaper
- cardboard pieces
- bubble wrap
- plastic wrap
- aluminum foil
- hard-boiled eggs

LITERACY CONNECTIONS

Humpty Dumpty Climbs Again
by Dave Horowitz

Humpty Dumpty
by Daniel Kirk

NOTES

STEAM
—IN—
ACTION

DILEMMA   ENGAGE

Read aloud *Humpty Dumpty Climbs Again* by Dave Horowitz.

Humpty's friends need his help! But ever since his fall in front of all the king's horses and all the king's men, Humpty has been feeling embarrassed and doesn't want to come out of his house. He is afraid of falling to pieces again and doesn't want to humiliate himself a second time. Humpty really wants to help his friends, but he knows how fragile and clumsy he is. Humpty needs your help in building a device that will keep him safe in case he accidentally falls again.

MISSION

Build a device that will keep Humpty from cracking when he falls from a distance of at least 4 ft.

BLUEPRINT   EXPLORE

Provide the Individual and Group Blueprint Design Sheets to engineering teams. Have individual students sketch a prototype to present to the other members of their team. Teams will discuss the pros and cons of each sketch and then select one prototype to construct.

ENGINEERING TASK	TEST TRIAL	ANALYZE	REDESIGN
Each team will construct a device that will protect an egg when dropped from a height of 4 ft.	Each team will test its prototype by placing an egg inside it and dropping it from a height of 4 ft. Teams will record observations about the results of each team's trial. If teams are successful with the drop at 4 ft., drop the eggs from a greater height. *Note:* Place plastic wrap or newspaper under the egg drop location for easy clean up.	Teams will analyze their results. Have students discuss some of the more successful design features with the class. Teams should be allowed to observe the other designs to gather ideas, reflect, and make changes in order to improve their prototypes.	Teams can use a colored pencil to make adjustments to their original design sketches. Then they can get new supplies if needed to rebuild and retest their prototypes.

 HELPFUL TIPS

- After the Test Trial, have teams take a gallery walk to view other teams' designs for possible ideas to assist them in the Analyze and Redesign portions of the engineering design process.

- If teams are successful on the first try, encourage them to make their prototypes even more efficient. If it is a scenario in which this is not feasible, distribute team members to other teams to be a support for them in making their prototypes more efficient. Alternatively, at teacher discretion, move students on to the Justification portion of the lesson.

- If after the third test the final prototype is still unsuccessful, have students write how they would start over. These challenges are meant to have students build on what they originally designed. If the design proved to be unsuccessful, encourage a reflection or justification on what they would do if they were allowed to start again from scratch.

REFLECTIONS — EXPLAIN & ELABORATE

AFTER TEST TRIAL 1	Did your egg survive the fall without cracking? Did your prototype stay intact?
ANALYSIS	What parts of your design helped to protect the egg? What changes could you make to your prototype to make sure the egg is safe during the next fall?
AFTER TEST TRIAL 2	Did your egg and your prototype both stay intact after the fall? Did other prototypes work more effectively than yours?
ANALYSIS	What were some parts of other teams' prototypes that helped keep their eggs safe? Why did these designs work better than others?
AFTER TEST TRIAL 3	What part of your prototype could you change to keep the egg safe during a fall from a greater height? Which materials were most effective in this challenge?

JUSTIFICATION — EVALUATE

ELA	*Note:* Students will need a copy of the comic strip template on page 139. Write and illustrate a story from Humpty Dumpty's point of view. Describe his first adventure: leaving home with his new safety device.
ARTS	Create an advertisement for your safety contraption highlighting the design qualities that make your prototype effective and safe.

I SCREAM, YOU SCREAM

1-2 HOURS

TIME FOR COMPLETION

S t E A m

SETTING
— THE —
STAGE

DESIGN CHALLENGE PURPOSE

Determine which type of salt to use to make ice cream faster than the other teams.

TEACHER DEVELOPMENT

This lesson will focus on the concept of freezing and solutions. When talking about making ice cream, applying rock salt quickly lowers the freezing point of the liquid. When completing this challenge, the one variable that will change is the type of salt being added to the ice in the outer baggie. This will be determined by trial and error (teams testing their hypothesis). Teams will record their observations to determine which type of salt works best. Water freezes at 32° F. However, a mixture of water and salt freezes at a much lower rate. The outside baggie has ice and salt (a solution), causing a lower temperature to surround the inner bag solution of milk, sugar, and vanilla. This causes the heat in the inner bag to transfer to the outer bag and causes the inner bag solution to freeze, creating the ice cream.

STUDENT DEVELOPMENT

Students that live in places where it snows may be able to connect this activity to background knowledge they have gathered from observing salt being sprinkled on icy roads and sidewalks to cause the snow to melt. The salt lowers the freezing point of the water that would have turned to ice. What they may not understand is how that works successfully. Students need to understand that if you apply heat to certain solids, they have the potential to turn into liquids. And when heat is applied long enough, some solids can also turn from a solid to a liquid and finally to a gas. Conversely, when heat is removed from some liquids, they can turn to solids.

Lesson Idea: Ice Challenge! Provide an ice cube inside a cup to groups of students, and challenge them to make the ice melt the fastest. Do not provide hints about how to do it. You might see some groups blow hot breath on it. Some teams might shake the container to break the ice cube into smaller pieces that will melt much easier. What you are ultimately hoping to see is students using a heat source (e.g., blowing on it and holding it in their bare hands).

STANDARDS

SCIENCE	TECHNOLOGY	ENGINEERING	ARTS	MATH	ELA
2-PS1-1		K-2-ETS1-1	Creating #1		CCSS.ELA-LITERACY.W.2.4
2-PS1-4		K-2-ETS1-2	Creating #2		
		K-2-ETS1-3			

SCIENCE & ENGINEERING PRACTICES

Planning and Carrying Out Investigations: Plan and conduct an investigation collaboratively to produce data to serve as the basis for evidence to answer a question.

Analyzing and Interpreting Data: Analyze data from tests of an object or tool to determine if it works as intended.

Constructing Explanations and Designing Solutions: Make observations (firsthand or from media) to construct an evidence-based account for natural phenomena.

Engaging in Argument from Evidence: Construct an argument with evidence to support a claim.

CROSSCUTTING CONCEPTS

Patterns: Patterns in the natural and human-designed world can be observed.

Cause and Effect: Events have causes that generate observable patterns. Simple tests can be designed to gather evidence to support or refute student ideas about causes.

Energy and Matter: Objects may break into smaller pieces and be put together into larger pieces, or change shapes.

TARGET VOCABULARY

freezing point   volume

matter   weight

temperature

LITERACY CONNECTIONS

The Relatives Came
by Cynthia Rylant

I'm Hungry
by Josie Irene Swartz

A Visitor for Bear (Bear and Mouse)
by Bonny Becker

MATERIALS

- measuring spoons
- measuring cups
- spoons
- tape
- stopwatch
- sugar
- milk
- vanilla extract
- ice
- ice cream recipe (page 140)

Teams select one of the following types of salt:

- rock salt
- kosher salt
- table salt

Teams select two of the following to construct a container:

- small resealable plastic bag
- gallon-size resealable plastic bag
- small paper cup
- plastic grocery bag
- paper bag
- Styrofoam cup
- plastic cup

NOTES

STEAM
—IN—
ACTION

DILEMMA   ENGAGE

You just got a call that all of your relatives are coming to visit after dinner. They expect you to serve them dessert. Panicking, you look in the refrigerator and the pantry, searching for something to make. There are only a few items that you can turn into a tasty dessert. You decide to make ice cream! You read through your ice cream recipe and discover that it doesn't say what kind of container to mix the ingredients in or what kind of salt to use. Ice cream takes awhile to make, and you don't have much time. Use the materials provided to make ice cream as fast as possible.

MISSION

Select the best container and type of salt to make ice cream faster than the other teams.

BLUEPRINT   EXPLORE

After students have had time to research the use of salt to make ice cream, provide the Individual and Group Blueprint Design Sheets to engineering teams. Have individual students sketch a prototype of the ice cream container, determine which type of salt to use, and then present that information to the other members of their team. Teams will discuss the pros and cons of each suggestion. Then teams will select one prototype container to construct and which type of salt to use.

ENGINEERING TASK **TEST TRIAL** **ANALYZE** **REDESIGN**

ENGINEERING TASK	TEST TRIAL	ANALYZE	REDESIGN
Each team will choose the best materials to construct a container and the type of salt that will help make ice cream the fastest. *Note:* Before starting the stopwatch at the beginning of each test trial, the teacher will take and record the temperature of the materials inside each team's container. This process will be repeated for each test trial once the stopwatch is stopped.	Teams will follow the ice cream recipe and add the type of salt they think will make the ice cold enough to turn the liquid ingredients into solid ice cream. Time the trial from the point the bag closes and teams start shaking it until a team has a product that changed from a liquid to a complete solid.	Teams should be allowed to observe the other container designs and salt choices to gather ideas, reflect, and make changes in order to improve their results.	Teams can attempt another trial after reviewing the class results from trial one. They need to first analyze the class data and their trial one data, then determine if the salt they chose worked as well as the salt used by other groups. Teams also need to determine if the materials they used for the container played a part in the effectiveness of their prototypes.

 HELPFUL TIPS

- After the Test Trial, have teams take a gallery walk to view other teams' designs for possible ideas to assist them in the Analyze and Redesign portions of the engineering design process.

- If teams are successful on the first try, encourage them to make their prototypes even more efficient. If it is a scenario in which this is not feasible, distribute team members to other teams to be a support for them in making their prototypes more efficient. Alternatively, at teacher discretion, move students on to the Justification portion of the lesson.

- If after the third test the final prototype is still unsuccessful, have students write how they would start over. These challenges are meant to have students build on what they originally designed. If the design proved to be unsuccessful, encourage a reflection or justification on what they would do if they were allowed to start again from scratch.

REFLECTIONS — EXPLAIN & ELABORATE

AFTER TEST TRIAL 1	Teams will compare their container materials and salt choices to those used by other teams.
ANALYSIS	After comparing their freezing time to that of the other groups, teams should discuss why they believe their time was good or needed improvement. Teams will be able to view other teams' types of salt and the containers that they used.
AFTER TEST TRIAL 2	Teams will compare their container materials and salt choices to other teams as well as to their first test results.
ANALYSIS	Teams need to calculate their temperature changes and compare them to the temperature changes of the other groups to determine if the salt type and/or the container type caused the temperature to drop faster or not.
AFTER TEST TRIAL 3	Teams need to analyze the temperature changes and the time that it took the ice cream to freeze. After looking at the three data sets, they should determine if the changes they made were positive. They should determine what type of salt and container was the best for making ice cream the fastest.

JUSTIFICATION — EVALUATE

ELA	*Note:* Students will need a copy of the story reproducible on page 141. After eating your ice cream, write a story about how you created ice cream in time for your family's visit.
ARTS	Create a jingle for fast-freezing ice cream.

I'M FREEZING!

3-4 HOURS
TIME FOR COMPLETION

SETTING —THE— STAGE

DESIGN CHALLENGE PURPOSE

Design and construct a prototype of a cooler cup that keeps ice solid for the longest period of time.

TEACHER DEVELOPMENT

This challenge is designed for students to explore solid and liquid states of **matter**. Students will need to know those two states of matter prior to completing this challenge.

A **liquid** is a state of matter which takes the shape of the container it is in. A **solid** has a definite shape. The challenge focuses on the concept of slowing down the change of a solid into a liquid.

STUDENT DEVELOPMENT

Students will need an understanding of solid and liquid states of matter. Prior to beginning this lesson, it is advisable that students participate in an observation of ice melting. Discuss why ice melts outside of a freezer or ice chest. Talk about how the temperature of the air surrounding the ice cube is warmer than the temperature of the ice cube. This causes the ice to melt. Ask students whether or not there is a way to reverse the process and turn the liquid back into solid ice. Discuss how that happens.

STANDARDS

SCIENCE	TECHNOLOGY	ENGINEERING	ARTS	MATH	ELA
2-PS1-1		K-2-ETS1-1	Creating #1	CCSS.MATH. CONTENT.2.NBT.B.6	CCSS.ELA-LITERACY.SL.2.1.B
2-PS1-4		K-2-ETS1-2			CCSS.ELA-LITERACY.W.2.6
		K-2-ETS1-3			

SCIENCE & ENGINEERING PRACTICES

Asking Questions and Defining Problems: Define a simple problem that can be solved through the development of a new or improved object or tool.

Developing and Using Models: Develop a simple model based on evidence to represent a proposed object or tool.

Constructing Explanations and Designing Solutions: Use tools and/or materials to design and/or build a device that solves a specific problem or a solution to a specific problem.

CROSSCUTTING CONCEPTS

Cause and Effect: Simple tests can be designed to gather evidence to support or refute student ideas about causes.

Energy and Matter: Flows, Cycles, and Conservation—Objects may change shape.

TARGET VOCABULARY

engineer

liquid

matter

prototype

solid

MATERIALS

- ice cubes
- aluminum foil
- masking tape
- newspaper
- paper plates
- rubber bands
- paper cups (waxed cups will last longer)
- wax paper
- stopwatch

LITERACY CONNECTIONS

Change It!: Solids Liquids, and Gases by Adrienne Mason

NOTES

STEAM
— IN —
ACTION

DILEMMA   ENGAGE

Mr. Icee, president of Iceworld Coolers, discovered that a competitor has developed a new cup that will keep ice solid even longer than his Iceworld products! Mr. Icee wants to make sure he has a similar product to offer his customers, but he is not sure how to do it.

Mr. Icee needs you to help him design his next great product! Use the materials provided to create a cooler cup prototype that keeps ice in a solid state for the longest period of time. Can you help Mr. Icee?

MISSION

Construct a cooler cup prototype that will keep ice solid for the longest period of time. The team that meets the challenge will choose the name of Mr. Icee's new cooler cup!

BLUEPRINT   EXPLORE

Provide the Individual and Group Blueprint Design Sheets to engineering teams. Have individual students sketch a prototype to present to the other members of their team. Teams will discuss the pros and cons of each sketch and then select one prototype to construct.

ENGINEERING TASK   **TEST TRIAL**   **ANALYZE**   **REDESIGN**

ENGINEERING TASK	TEST TRIAL	ANALYZE	REDESIGN
Each engineering team will design a cooler cup.	Each team will test its prototype by placing a piece of ice inside and timing how long it takes to melt. Teams will record their observations. *Note:* This may take up to an hour.	Teams discuss the details of their designs with other teams to determine some of the more successful design features. Teams should be allowed to observe the other designs to gather ideas, reflect, and make changes in order to improve their prototypes.	Teams can use a colored pencil to make adjustments to their original design sketches. Then they can get new supplies if needed to rebuild and retest their prototypes.

 # HELPFUL TIPS

- After the Test Trial, have teams take a gallery walk to view other teams' designs for possible ideas to assist them in the Analyze and Redesign portions of the engineering design process.

- If teams are successful on the first try, encourage them to make their prototypes even more efficient. If it is a scenario in which this is not feasible, distribute team members to other teams to be a support for them in making their prototypes more efficient. Alternatively, at teacher discretion, move students on to the Justification portion of the lesson.

- If after the third test the final prototype is still unsuccessful, have students write how they would start over. These challenges are meant to have students build on what they originally designed. If the design proved to be unsuccessful, encourage a reflection or justification on what they would do if they were allowed to start again from scratch.

REFLECTIONS · EXPLAIN & ELABORATE

AFTER TEST TRIAL 1	How long did it take to melt the ice in your cup prototype? After looking at the other teams' prototypes, what part of your prototype would you like to adjust?
ANALYSIS	Explain how this change will make the ice take longer to melt.
AFTER TEST TRIAL 2	Did it take longer to melt the ice this time? Explain what part of the design made this possible.
ANALYSIS	What changes will you make to improve your prototype?
AFTER TEST TRIAL 3	Which team's prototype was the most effective? Why do you think that cooler cup kept ice solid the longest?
ANALYSIS	If you could start over, what would you do differently? Why?

JUSTIFICATION · EVALUATE

ELA	Write a jingle or slogan for a commercial to advertise your cooler cup. Ask yourself, *Why should customers buy my prototype instead of my competitors' cup?*
ARTS	Create a poster to advertise your cooler cup and convince Mr. Icee to choose your prototype.

TAKE APART AND BUILD ANEW

STEAM

SETTING —THE— STAGE

DESIGN CHALLENGE PURPOSE

Turn the pieces from a large house into two separate houses for Hansel and Gretel.

TEACHER DEVELOPMENT

Students will need to understand that large objects made up of smaller pieces can be disassembled and made into new objects using the original pieces. For this challenge, you will need to build a large model of a house. You can use graham crackers and icing, blocks, or other objects that can be used to build a three-dimensional model.

This will be used as the display model during the challenge. You should construct this model prior to beginning the challenge. The model house must be made of the exact materials that you will give to teams to construct their own models. Providing teams with the exact same number, type, and size of materials used in your model is crucial.

STUDENT DEVELOPMENT

Shapes can be partitioned, or divided, into halves and fourths. For example, a rectangle can be divided in half to create two equal-sized rectangles smaller than the original single rectangle. This challenge requires students to build two model houses using the pieces taken from a larger model house.

Lesson Idea: Give student pairs a hexagon pattern block and other pattern block shapes. Have each student pair recreate a hexagon using the other pattern blocks.

STANDARDS

SCIENCE	TECHNOLOGY	ENGINEERING	ARTS	MATH	ELA
2-PS1-3		K-2-ETS1-1	Creating #1	CCSS.MATH. CONTENT.2.G.A.3	CCSS.ELA- LITERACY.W.2.3
		K-2-ETS1-2	Creating #2		
		K-2-ETS1-3			

SCIENCE & ENGINEERING PRACTICES

Constructing Explanations and Designing Solutions: Make observations (firsthand or from media) to construct an evidence-based account for natural phenomena.

CROSSCUTTING CONCEPTS

Energy and Matter: Objects may break into smaller pieces and be put together into larger pieces, or change shapes.

TARGET VOCABULARY

identical

partitioned

recycled

LITERACY CONNECTIONS

The Missing Piece
by Shel Silverstein

MATERIALS

- cardboard (for a flat building surface)

Suggested Building Materials:

- square-bottomed milk cartons
- icing
- graham crackers
- pretzels
- gum drops
- building blocks
- tangrams
- other small objects to create the houses

Note: Teachers can build the large model out of their preferred materials. These exact materials will be given to each student team.

NOTES

STEAM IN ACTION

DILEMMA ENGAGE

Once upon a time, Hansel and Gretel went on a walk deep into the forest and discovered a large, abandoned gingerbread house. They decided that, since no one lived there, they would take the house apart so they could use the materials to build something new. Hansel and Gretel decided to build two new identical houses using these recycled materials. But they need your help! Can you design a blueprint for the two identical houses and then build models using all of the materials provided?

MISSION

Build two identical houses using all of the materials provided.

BLUEPRINT EXPLORE

Give each team a bag of the materials they will use for this challenge. Allow teams to look at the materials before filling out their Blueprint Design Sheets.

Provide the Individual and Group Blueprint Design Sheets to engineering teams. Have individual students sketch a prototype to present to the other members of their team. Teams will discuss the pros and cons of each sketch and then select one prototype to construct.

Note: Immediately after reading the dilemma aloud, show students the large model house you prepared in advance.

ENGINEERING TASK	TEST TRIAL	ANALYZE	REDESIGN
Each team will use the same materials used in the construction of the large house model to build two separate but identical houses.	Teams will determine whether or not they were able to create two complete houses using all of the materials.	Teams should be allowed to observe the other designs to gather ideas, reflect, and make changes in order to improve their models.	Teams can use a colored pencil to make adjustments to their original design sketches. Then they can get new supplies if needed to rebuild and retest their prototypes

HELPFUL TIPS

- After the Test Trial, have teams take a gallery walk to view other teams' designs for possible ideas to assist them in the Analyze and Redesign portions of the engineering design process.

- If teams are successful on the first try, encourage them to make their prototypes even more efficient. If it is a scenario in which this is not feasible, distribute team members to other teams to be a support for them in making their prototypes more efficient. Alternatively, at teacher discretion, move students on to the Justification portion of the lesson.

- If after the third test the final prototype is still unsuccessful, have students write how they would start over. These challenges are meant to have students build on what they originally designed. If the design proved to be unsuccessful, encourage a reflection or justification on what they would do if they were allowed to start again from scratch.

REFLECTIONS — EXPLAIN & ELABORATE

AFTER TEST TRIAL 1	Do your two new houses look the same? Did you use all of the pieces provided?
ANALYSIS	What change can you make to your houses to make them look the same?
AFTER TEST TRIAL 2	Did the changes make the houses identical? Did you use all of the materials you were given? Can you identify the pieces used in your two houses that were also used to build the larger model?
ANALYSIS	What can you change to ensure that your two houses look alike and that you are using all the pieces?
AFTER TEST TRIAL 3	Did you use all of the materials? Are the houses identical? What changes can you make so that two houses are exactly the same for Hansel and Gretel?

JUSTIFICATION — EVALUATE

ELA	Write a story about Hansel and Gretel finding the large graham cracker house in the forest. Use temporal words and phrases, such as *first*, *then*, and *finally* to signal event order.
ARTS	Place your houses together with the houses of other teams to make a village. Create trees and other details for the village.

APPENDIX

STEAM Design Challenges Gr. 2 © 2017 Creative Teaching Press

★ WANTED ★

WANTED FOR: _____

LAST SEEN: _____

IF FOUND, CONTACT: _____

REWARD: _____

THIS MODEL FLOWS! – RUBRIC

REQUIREMENTS	0 POINTS	1 POINT	2 POINTS
Lake	There is no lake.	There is a lake that pools. It is not labeled.	There is a lake that pools, and it is labeled correctly on the map.
River	There is no river.	There is a river that flows into a body of water. It is not labeled.	There is a river that flows into a body of water, and it is labeled correctly on the map.
Canyon	There is no canyon.	There is a canyon with steep sides that has water flowing through it. It is not labeled.	There is a canyon with steep sides that has water flowing through it, and it is labeled correctly on the map.
Waterfall	There is no waterfall.	There is a waterfall that has water flowing from a high place to a lower place. It is not labeled.	There is a waterfall that has water flowing from a high place to a lower place, and it is labeled correctly on the map.
Map	There is no map.	The map is incorrectly labeled.	The map has all of the required labels, and it accurately represents the model.

TOTAL

STEAM Design Challenges Gr. 2 © 2017 Creative Teaching Press

MAP OF THE RIDE

_____

(Name of log chute ride)

EXTRA! EXTRA!

PROTECT OUR
BEES

By _____

_____

_____

_____

_____

HABITAT RUBRIC

	1	2	3
Habitat Research Graphic Organizer	Research sheet is incomplete or contains some incorrect information. Work is not written neatly.	Research sheet is mostly filled out. Work is written neatly.	Research sheet is filled out completely. Work is written neatly.
Teamwork	Team did not work well together.	Team worked well together most of the time.	Team worked well together the entire time.
Diorama	Diorama includes only 2 plants or animals from the habitat.	Diorama includes at least 3 plants or animals from the habitat.	Diorama includes at least 4 plants or animals from the habitat.
Effort	Team showed little or no effort throughout the challenge.	Team showed some effort throughout the challenge.	Team showed lots of effort throughout the challenge.

TOTAL

HABITAT RESEARCH OUTLINE

Name of habitat: _____

Animals in this habitat:

1. _____

2. _____

3. _____

4. _____

Plants in this habitat:

1. _____

2. _____

3. _____

4. _____

Interesting facts:

1. _____

_____

2. _____

_____

3. _____

_____

⚙ A DAY IN THE LIFE OF ⚙

_____

By _____

_____

_____

_____

_____

_____

_____

_____

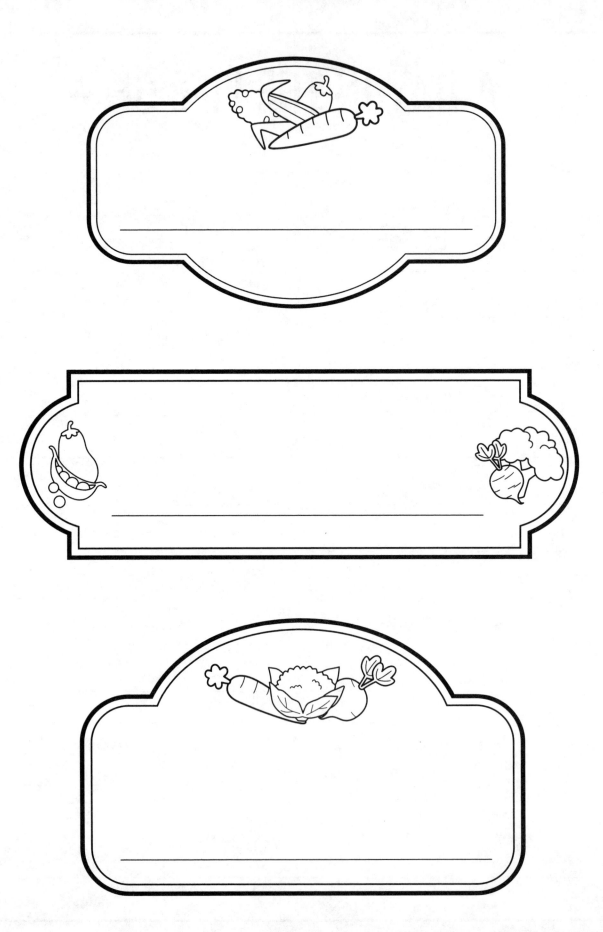

ANIMAL RESEARCH OUTLINE

Name of Animal #1: _____

Animal habitat: _____

How does the animal move seeds?

_____

_____

Two interesting facts about the animal:

1. _____

2. _____

ANIMAL RESEARCH OUTLINE

Name of Animal #2: _____

Animal habitat: _____

How does the animal move seeds?

_____

_____

Two interesting facts about the animal:

1. _____

2. _____

ANIMAL RUBRIC

	1	2	3
Animal Prototype	The animal is not easy to identify.	The animal is easy to identify, but the team is not able to describe how its animal transports seeds from a parent plant to another area.	The animal is easy to identify. The team is able to explain how its animal transports seeds from a parent plant to another area in at least two ways.
Seed Dispersal Q & A	Team is not successful at creating an easily identifiable animal and cannot, therefore, explain how its animal would transport and disperse seeds.	Team members are not able to answer questions regarding their animal's ability to transport and disperse seeds beyond the initial explanation.	Team members are able to answer questions regarding their animal's ability to transport and disperse seeds. They can give examples of how this happens.

TOTAL

STEAM Design Challenges Gr. 2 © 2017 Creative Teaching Press

COMIC STRIP

MIDDLE

END

BEGINNING

GLUE

RECIPE

— BEST EVER — HOMEMADE ICE CREAM

INGREDIENTS:

½ cup milk　　　½ cup salt

½ teaspoon vanilla　4 cups crushed ice

1 tablespoon sugar

DIRECTIONS:

Place ingredients in a container and seal it. Place the sealed container inside a second container filled with salt and ice. Close the container. Shake until the mixture changes from a liquid to a solid.

RECIPE

— BEST EVER — HOMEMADE ICE CREAM

INGREDIENTS:

½ cup milk　　　½ cup salt

½ teaspoon vanilla　4 cups crushed ice

1 tablespoon sugar

DIRECTIONS:

Place ingredients in a container and seal it. Place the sealed container inside a second container filled with salt and ice. Close the container. Shake until the mixture changes from a liquid to a solid.

RECIPE

— BEST EVER — HOMEMADE ICE CREAM

INGREDIENTS:

½ cup milk　　　½ cup salt

½ teaspoon vanilla　4 cups crushed ice

1 tablespoon sugar

DIRECTIONS:

Place ingredients in a container and seal it. Place the sealed container inside a second container filled with salt and ice. Close the container. Shake until the mixture changes from a liquid to a solid.

RECIPE

— BEST EVER — HOMEMADE ICE CREAM

INGREDIENTS:

½ cup milk　　　½ cup salt

½ teaspoon vanilla　4 cups crushed ice

1 tablespoon sugar

DIRECTIONS:

Place ingredients in a container and seal it. Place the sealed container inside a second container filled with salt and ice. Close the container. Shake until the mixture changes from a liquid to a solid.

SURPRISE FAMILY DESSERT

By _____

_____

_____

_____

_____

_____

_____

_____

_____

_____

_____

_____

TEAM MEMBER NAMES	PROS OF DESIGN	CONS OF DESIGN

GROUP BLUEPRINT DESIGN SHEET

TEAM REASONING

_____

_____

_____

_____

_____

_____

_____

TEACHER APPROVAL:

⚙️ BUDGET PLANNING CHART ⚙️

TITLE:

MATERIALS	COST	1st TEST TRIAL		2nd TEST TRIAL		3rd TEST TRIAL	
		ITEM(S)	AMOUNT	ITEM(S)	AMOUNT	ITEM(S)	AMOUNT
TOTAL COST:							

STEAM JOB CARDS

Construction Specialist

Description: This person is the one whose design was chosen. This person builds the prototype and is responsible for ensuring that the prototype follows the design rules exactly.

Material Resource Officer

Description: This person is in charge of getting, measuring, and cutting materials for the prototype. This person assists the construction specialist by getting materials ready and assisting in construction.

Engineering Supervisor

Description: This person is the team leader. This person assists all other team members as needed. This person acts as spokesperson for the team. This person will test the team's prototype.

Administrative Contractor

Description: This person is responsible for overseeing the construction specialist. This person must measure or otherwise ensure that prototype construction matches the blueprint design.

(Use only with groups of five.)

Accounts Manager

Description: This person holds the purse strings, keeps the team's finance records (budget sheet), and pays for all materials. This person assists the engineering supervisor with testing and recording all data.

Description:

My Inventor's Notebook

_____
Name

STEAM MONEY

STEAM MONEY

STEAM DESIGN CHALLENGES TEAM RUBRIC

	EXEMPLARY	PROFICIENT	PROGRESSING	BEGINNING
DESIGN	Team members reach consensus as to which prototype to construct. They complete team blueprint design sheet in which they include their reasons for selecting the team prototype. They include a written explanation to compare and contrast the prototypes they sketched individually. Prototype is constructed according to specifications in the team blueprint design.	Team members reach consensus as to which prototype to construct. They include their reasons for selecting the prototype but do not include a written explanation to compare and contrast the prototypes they sketched individually. Prototype is constructed according to the specifications in the team blueprint design.	Team members reach consensus as to which prototype to construct. They include their reasons for selecting the prototype but do not include a written explanation to compare and contrast the prototypes they sketched individually. Prototype is not constructed according to the specifications of the blueprint design.	Team members reach consensus as to which prototype to construct. They do not include either their reasons for selecting the prototype or a written explanation to compare and contrast the prototypes they sketched. Prototype is constructed.
TEST	Teams test their prototype. They record observations that align with the design challenge. They make note of any unique design flaws.	Teams test their prototype and record observations that align with the design challenge.	Teams test their prototype. They record observations that do not align with the design challenge.	Teams test their prototype. They do not record observations.

STEAM DESIGN CHALLENGES TEAM RUBRIC

	EXEMPLARY	PROFICIENT	PROGRESSING	BEGINNING
ANALYZE	Team members participate in an analytic discussion about their testing and observations. They reflect on their design as compared to at least three other teams. They discuss their intended redesign steps, defending their reasoning in their discussion.	Team members participate in an analytic discussion about their testing and observations. They reflect on their design as compared to at least two other teams. They discuss their intended redesign steps.	Team members participate in an analytic discussion about their testing and observations, comparing their design with at least one other team's. They discuss their intended redesign steps.	Team members participate in an analytic discussion about their testing but do not compare their design with another team's. They discuss their intended redesign steps.
REDESIGN	Team redesigns its prototype. Original sketch is altered using a colored pencil to illustrate changes made with supporting reasons.	Team redesigns its prototype. Original sketch is altered using a colored pencil to illustrate changes made.	Team redesigns its prototype. Original sketch is altered to illustrate changes made.	Team redesigns its prototype.
EVALUATE	Team completes a justification activity. Team reflects and makes meaningful connections to the science standards as well as to two of the other STEAM standards addressed in the lesson.	Team completes a justification activity. Team reflects and makes meaningful connections to the science standards as well as to one of the other STEAM standards addressed in the lesson.	Team completes a justification activity. Team reflects and makes meaningful connections to the science standards addressed in the lesson.	Team completes a justification activity. Team makes no connection to the science standards addressed in the lesson.

BIBLIOGRAPHY

"All About States of Matter." Easy Science for Kids. Accessed August 29, 2016.
http://easyscienceforkids.com/all-about-states-of-matter/.

"Barrier Islands and Sea Level Rise." Teach Ocean Science. University of Maryland Center for Environmental Science. Accessed August 28, 2016. http://teachoceanscience.net/teaching_resources/education_modules/barrier_islands_and_sea_level_rise/learn/.

"Catapult." Discovery Kids. Accessed August 29, 2016.
http://discoverykids.com/games/catapult/.

Collins, Donna. *Habitats*. Accessed September 2, 2016.
http://zunal.com/webquest.php?w=54297.

"Cool Sites for Kids." Penn State College of Agricultural Sciences. Department of Entomology. Accessed September 5, 2016. http://ento.psu.edu/public/kids/cool-sites-for-kids.

"Dispersal of Seeds by Animals." The Seed Site. Accessed August 29, 2016.
http://the seedsite.co.uk/sdanimal.html.

Emery, David. "Apicalypse Now." Snopes. Accessed September 3, 2016.
http://www.snopes.com/zika-spraying-kills-millions-of-bees/.

"The Great Plant Escape." University of Illinois Extension. Accessed September 5, 2016. http://extension.illinois.edu/gpe/index.cfm.

"Habitats/Biomes." Enchanted Learning. Accessed September 2, 2016.
http://www.enchantedlearning.com/biomes/.

"How Does Static Electricity Work?" Everyday Mysteries: Fun Science Facts from the Library of Congress. Accessed September 3, 2016. https://www.loc.gov/rr/scitech/mysteries/static.html.

"How to Grow Lima Beans." Grow This! Accessed August 28, 2016.
http://www.growthis.com/how-to-grow-lima-beans/.

"Hurricanes." Weather Wiz Kids. Accessed August 28, 2016.
http://www.weatherwizkids.com/weather-hurricane.htm.

"Insects." Bugfacts.net. Accessed September 5, 2016. http://www.bugfacts.net/insects.php.

"Insects." Easy Science for Kids. Accessed September 5, 2016.
http://easyscienceforkids.com/animals/insects/.

Kansas City Star. Adapted by Newsela Staff. *After a Concussion, When Can Teens Return to the Football Field?* Accessed September 5, 2016. https://newsela.com/articles/concussion-kids/id/5734/.

Lawrence, Timothy. *Pollination and Protecting Bees and Other Pollinators*.
Washington State University Extension. Accessed September 3, 2016.
http://cru.cahe.wsu.edu/CEPublications/FS174E/FS174E.pdf.

Long, Melinda. "How I Became a Pirate." *Read aloud* by Paul Cuthbert.
Accessed August 28, 2016. https://www.youtube.com/watch?v=y4m_BW5yddU.

"Physical Map of the United States." U.S. Department of Homeland Security. Accessed August 28, 2016.
https://www.ready.gov/translations/spanish/america/_downloads/KidsPoster_Jan2011_map_web.pdf.

"Pollination." *Biology of Plants*. Missouri Botanical Garden. Accessed September 3, 2016.
http://www.mbgnet.net/bioplants/pollination.html.

"Southeastern U.S. Map." Freeworldmaps.net. Accessed August 28, 2016.
http://www.freeworldmaps.net/united-states/southeast/southeastern-us-map.jpg.

"States of Matter." BrainPOP. Accessed August 29, 2016.
https://www.brainpop.com/science/matterandchemistry/statesofmatter/.

STEAM Design Challenges Gr. 2 © 2017 Creative Teaching Press